XC

KU-300-156

Rotate

740004431468

WITHDRAWN AND
SOLD BY
HEREFORDSHIRE LIBRARIES

Chic & Unique
beaded
JEWELLERY

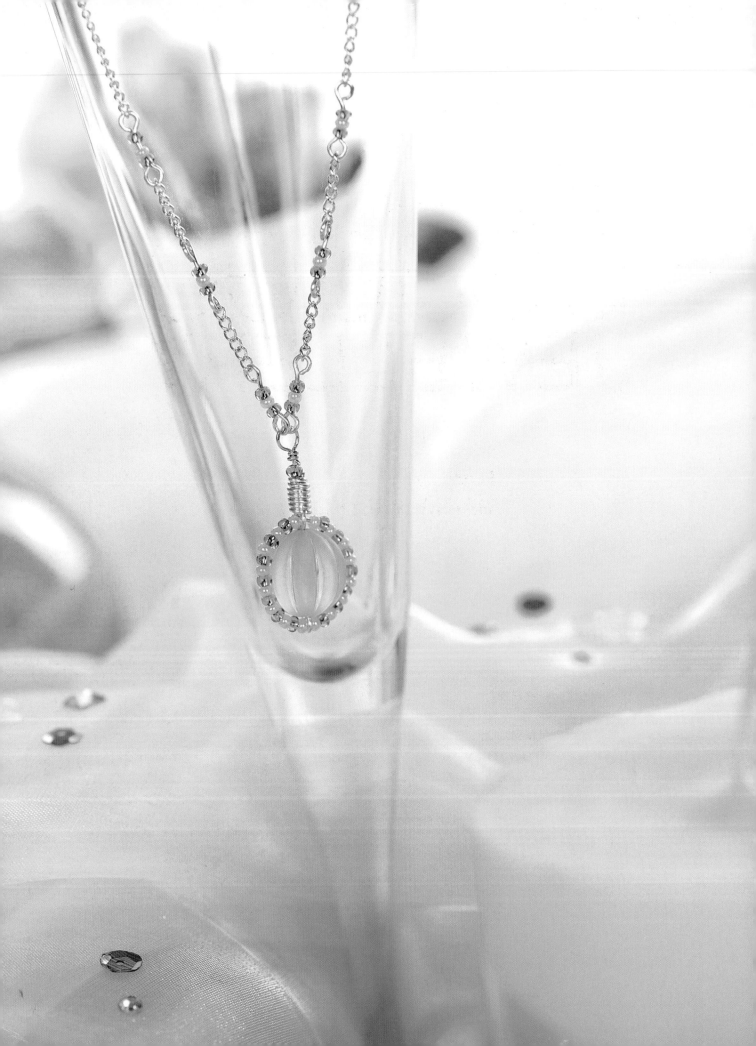

Chic & Unique
beaded
JEWELLERY

Edited by
NAOMI ABEYKOON

D&C
David and Charles

A DAVID & CHARLES BOOK
Copyright © David & Charles Limited 2007

David & Charles is an F+W Publications Inc.
company 4700 East Galbraith Road
Cincinnati, OH 45236

First published in the UK in 2007

Text and photographs copyright ©
Crafts Beautiful 2007

Crafts Beautiful and *Quick & Crafty* have asserted
their right to be identified as authors of this
work in accordance with the Copyright,
Designs and Patents Act, 1988.

All rights reserved. No part of this publication
may be reproduced, stored in a retrieval
system, or transmitted, in any form or by any
means, electronic or mechanical, by
photocopying, recording or otherwise, without
prior permission in writing from the publisher.

The designs in this book are copyright and
must not be made for resale.

The authors and publisher have made every
effort to ensure that all the instructions in the
book are accurate and safe, and therefore
cannot accept liability for any resulting injury,
damage or loss to persons or property,
however it may arise.

Names of manufacturers, bead ranges
and other products are provided for the
information of readers, with no intention
to infringe copyright or trademarks.

A catalogue record for this book is available
from the British Library.

ISBN-13: 978-0-7153-2727-2 paperback
ISBN-10: 0-7153-2727-5 paperback

Printed in China by SNP Leefung
for David & Charles
Brunel House   Newton Abbot   Devon

Commissioning Editor Jane Trollope
Desk Editor Bethany Dymond
Designers Emma Sandquest and Lisa Wyman
Project Editor Natasha Reed
Production Editor Sarah Crosland
Production Controller Ros Napper
Photographers Paul Barker and Anthony Jones

Visit our website at www.davidandcharles.co.uk

David & Charles books are available from all
good bookshops; alternatively you can contact
our Orderline on 0870 9908222 or write to us at
FREEPOST EX2 110, D&C Direct, Newton Abbot,
TQ12 4ZZ (no stamp required UK only);
US customers call 800-289-0963 and
Canadian customers call 800-840-5220.

The publisher would like to thank Naomi Abeykoon from
Crafts Beautiful for all her hard work and Dorothy Wood
for writing and compiling the front section of the book.

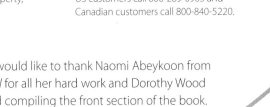

HEREFORDSHIRE LIBRARIES	
146	
Bertrams	13.12.07
745.594	£12.99

Contents

Super Sparkle

Funky Beads

Iced Gems

Pearly Power

Introduction

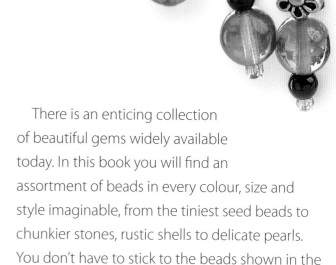

Create a wealth of beautiful beaded jewellery and gift items to treat yourself or someone special. Here you will find something to please everybody, with a sparkling collection of 55 stunning jewellery projects, brought to you by a host of talented designers. Be inspired to make beautifully ornate, head-turning accessories at a fraction of the price of shop-bought equivalents, with the added enjoyment that beading can bring!

Beading is a traditional craft that, over the last few years, has become one of the most popular hobbies. This huge resurgence has been due in part to current fashion trends resulting in department stores and shops stocking lots of gorgeous beaded items such as bags, shoes, clothes, household goods and gifts. Manufacturers are now producing more fashionable colours and shapes of beads and bead outlets are busier than ever.

There is an enticing collection of beautiful gems widely available today. In this book you will find an assortment of beads in every colour, size and style imaginable, from the tiniest seed beads to chunkier stones, rustic shells to delicate pearls. You don't have to stick to the beads shown in the

designs either – why not use this opportunity to recycle leftover beads or use anything that catches your eye to create a truly unique accessory that you will be proud to wear.

If you are new to beading, read through the first few pages of the book to learn a little about the innumerable sizes, colours and finishes of glass beads.

All the basic techniques that you will need are explained in detail, with helpful step-by-step photography to guide you along your way. Learn about beading knots and stitches, cutting and bending wire, using fastenings and much more. Useful patterns and diagrams are also included on pages 118–119 to provide additional help in making up the projects.

The bead projects in this book are divided into four sections. Super Sparkle will introduce you to a range of dazzling and glitzy jewellery, striking watch designs and a beautiful tiara, fit for a princess. Funky Beads is full of bling, with a range of highly glamorous bead-encrusted jewellery and sophisticated accessories, with influences from ethnic and boho styles to the Orient. Iced Gems brings the coolest designs in luscious blues and greens, while Pearly Power introduces a range of elegant and luxurious jewellery designs for that extra-special look, with delicate shells and beautiful beads.

All the projects in the book have clear instructions and list the colours and sizes of the beads used so that you can substitute beads from your own supplies. If you are new to beading, or just want to recreate one of the projects exactly, the supplier details are given on page 120.

Whatever your level of expertise, this book will keep you inspired and beading for a long time to come. So what are you waiting for? Create something chic and unique today!

Materials and equipment

The equipment shown here is for your reference and you will not need everything before you begin the projects in the book. A set of three jewellery tools will be useful as a starting point and then buy other specialist items as required.

Jewellery tools – a basic set of jewellery tools includes round-nose pliers for making neat loops, flat-nose pliers – preferably the narrow tip version known as snipe-nose for general holding and manipulating of wire – and wire cutters. Domestic tools are too large for fine wirework, so do look for smaller specialist tools in a craft or bead shop.

Bead mat – textured mats are essential when working with beads. The fine pile prevents the beads from rolling about and you are able to pick the beads up onto a needle or wire straight off the mat.

Specialist tools – crimping pliers, split ring pliers and a bead reamer are useful tools for making jewellery but not essential for the beginner.

Needles – beading needles have a flat eye for threading through tiny bead holes. Size 10 is a good general needle and use size 13 for fine work. Other beading needles include big eye needles, ideal for threading ribbons through beads, or twisted wire needles that are easy to thread and have a collapsible eye.

Jewellery findings – these are all the metal bits that make beadwork into jewellery. You can buy most items in silver- or gold-plated or in pure metal, which are more expensive. Earring findings, clasps, fastenings, jump rings, bails and headpins are some of the items you might use. Everything you need is listed with each project and is available from bead and craft shops.

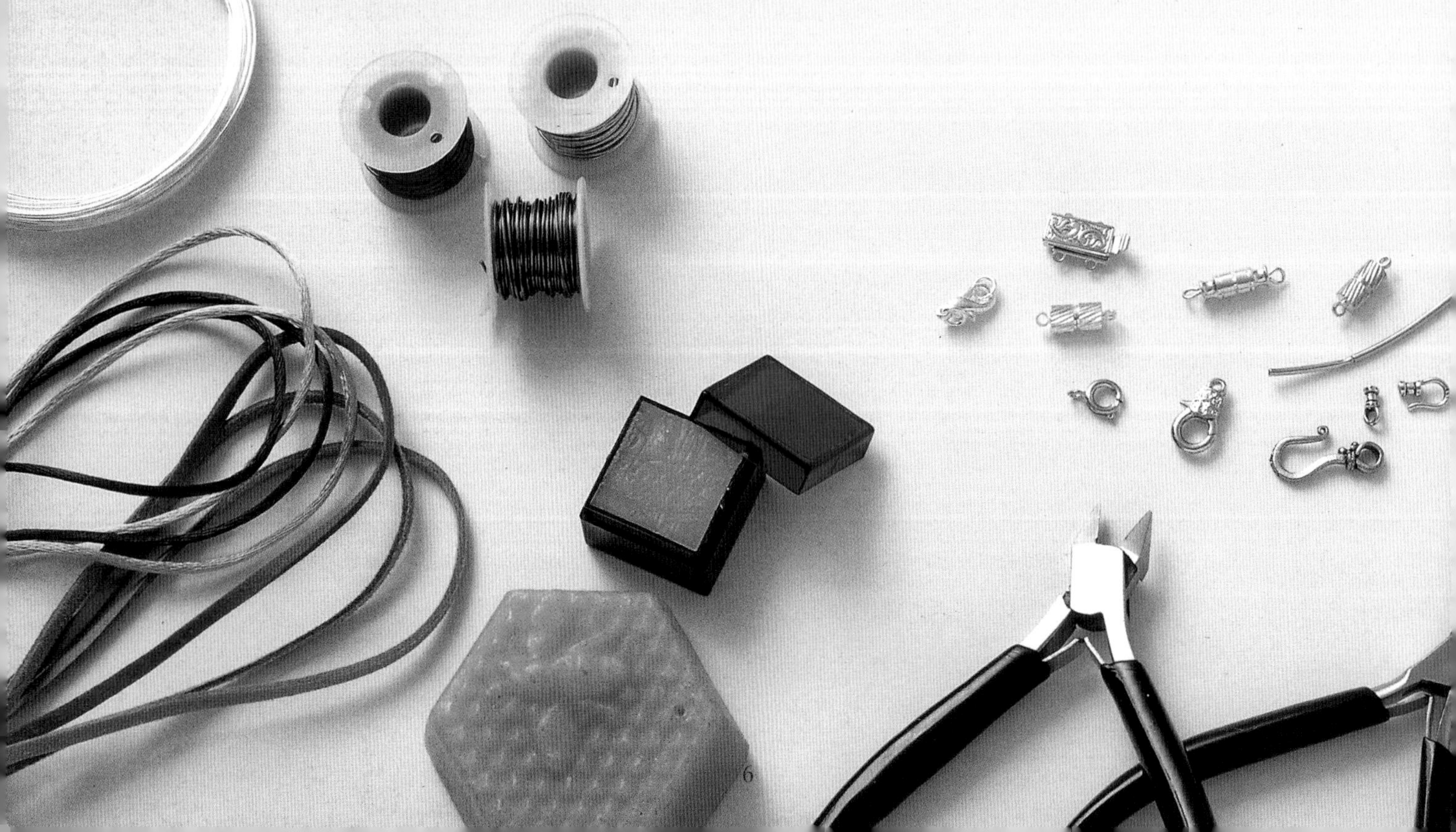

Wire and chain – craft and jewellery wire is generally copper based, with plating for silver and gold, or enamelling for a wide range of colours. Wire thickness is measured in millimetres or standard wire gauge (swg). Coated wires such as tigertail and softflex hold a soft curve and drape beautifully. Chain has become readily available in a wide range of styles, colours and weights.

Threads – multifilament threads such as Nymo™ and C-lon™ are ideal for bead stitching. C-lon™ is less prone to stretching and both come in a wide range of colours. Nylon or single filament threads are useful for bead stringing. Elastic thread, available in several thicknesses and colours, is ideal for simple bracelets.

Thread conditioner – beeswax or Thread Heaven™ are both used to condition threads. It is personal preference whether you use conditioners, which are designed to prevent knotting and tangling.

Thong, ribbon and cord – organza ribbon adds a delicate touch to jewellery projects. Cords vary in thickness from fine, waxed cords to the thicker silky rattail. Natural and man-made thong adds texture and colour to necklaces and bracelets.

Glues and adhesives – sticking beads and wire can be a little tricky because of their smooth surfaces. Use epoxy resin to add brooch backs or jewellery cement that stays soft once set and is ideal for securing knots.

Beads

Beads come in all shapes and sizes, from the tiniest seed beads to huge, chunky beads and are available from your local beading shop, on-line or by mail order. There are all sorts of beads, from cheap and cheerful plastic beads to more expensive semi-precious stones and high quality lamp beads, so you can always find something to suit the design and your pocket. Just remember that with beads you get what you pay for and inexpensive beads will be less even and of poorer quality. For something a little different try charity shops or car boot sales for old jewellery and other beaded items that can be recycled.

Bead types

Beads are available in a wide range of materials, from plastic and glass to natural materials such as wood, shell, bone, metal and semi-precious stones. Many glass beads have a finish to create different surface effects and not all are durable. Check before buying especially when making bracelets and necklaces where the beads rub against your wrist or neck.

Bead shapes and sizes

A quick look in any bead shop will reveal innumerable bead shapes and sizes. It is useful to know how the common bead shapes are measured, especially when buying from a catalogue or on-line as they are not always illustrated at their actual size.

Large beads are measured in millimetres; round beads are measured across the diameter and longer beads, like ovals, droplets and cylinders, are measured by length and width. Cubes and bicone beads, which look like two pyramids stuck together, are measured across the width.

Seed beads or rocailles are sold by size, from tiny petite beads (size 15) to larger pebble beads (size 3). Seed beads for general use are usually size 9, 10 or 11. Bugle beads, which are thin glass tubes, are sold by length.

Bead holes

All beads, unless they are a cabochon, have a hole of some sort to feed a thread, wire or cord through. The size of the hole varies and is not always in proportion to the size of the bead. It is a good idea to check the size especially if you are ordering beads from a catalogue or on-line. You can open out the hole in some beads using a bead reamer. Most bead holes are in the centre but you do get holes off-centre. Look closely at the photographs of the finished piece to see where the bead holes are positioned before you buy your beads.

Seed beads and bugles

Seed beads or rocailles are the names given to small glass beads, which come in a wide range of sizes, types and quality. Most of the highest quality beads are made in Japan and the Czech Republic and these are the most uniform in size and shape. Bugles are long cylinder-shaped beads made from rods of glass. They are available straight or twisted in lengths from a few millimetres to over 2.5cm and come in a range of colours and finishes like seed beads.

Pressed glass

Large glass beads are usually pressed in moulds to create lots of different shapes from leaves and flowers to discs, cylinders and drops. Transparent, brightly coloured glass beads will let the light through to keep your projects looking fresh and contemporary or try opaque darker shades for a more traditional look. Glass beads can have different finishes.

Crystals

Crystals are top quality faceted beads that sparkle beautifully when the light catches them. Top quality beads such as Swarovski crystals are expensive but look absolutely fabulous. On the other hand inexpensive faceted glass beads are ideal to make costume jewellery when quantity, rather than quality, ups the shine factor. Look out for wonderful crystal shapes, such as flowers, drops, hearts and cubes, all available in a wide range of colours and sizes.

Lampwork and decorative beads

There are a multitude of decorative glass beads including handmade lampwork beads with their distinctive lines of glass wound around the outside. Some beads have a silver or metallic lining that looks like leaf metal while others have a coloured lining or flecks of pattern in the glass.

Pearls

The lustre on pearls takes them into the luxury look even if the beads themselves can be inexpensive. Many 'pearls' are really just glass or plastic beads with a pearlised coating. Like every other type of bead the price varies with the quality and so you can make fun jewellery or buy fresh water or cultured pearls for something extra special.

Natural beads

Beads can be made from all sorts of natural materials such as shell, ivory, bone, bamboo and wood. Seeds and pods are simply drilled to create the bead and larger natural materials are carved to create the bead shape. Often natural beads come in their original colours but can also be dyed or painted.

Metal beads

As well as gold and silver, metal or metallic beads are available in other colours such as copper, bronze or pewter as well as antique finishes. Some metallic beads are actually painted plastic and have the advantage of a lighter weight. Metal spacers such as rings and washers are often used in between other beads or look for bead charms in shapes like hearts, shoes or even little handbags that add a fun touch.

Semi-precious beads

Semi-precious beads range from tiny irregular chips to very large balls and other shaped beads. These beads are often sold in strings and the price varies enormously depending on the stone and the quality. Many semi-precious beads come in a range of colours naturally, but some are dyed or heat treated to produce an assortment of different colours and shades.

Techniques

The basic techniques used for the jewellery projects in the book are illustrated with step-by-step photography. Diagrams are used to show how to work common knots and the two bead stitches featured.

Getting started

Jewellery making is one of the most satisfying crafts, as even a beginner can make stunning looking items suitable to keep or give as gifts. All of the projects have clear instructions but if you are new to jewellery making or want to try something new, refer to the techniques section before you start.

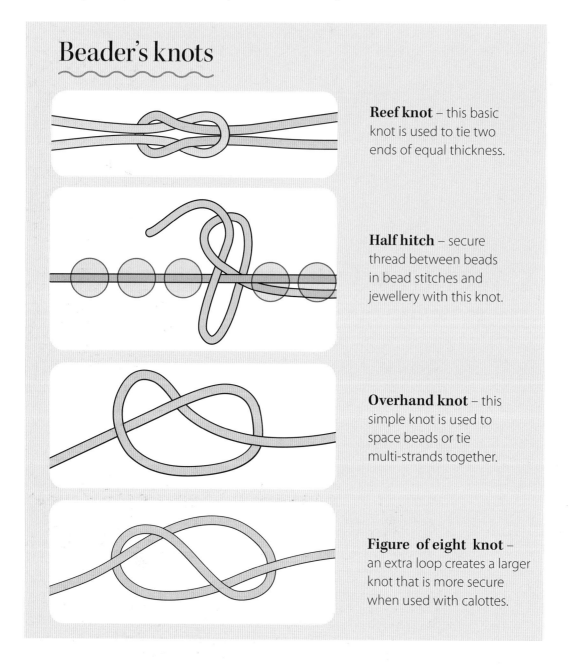

Beader's knots

Reef knot – this basic knot is used to tie two ends of equal thickness.

Half hitch – secure thread between beads in bead stitches and jewellery with this knot.

Overhand knot – this simple knot is used to space beads or tie multi-strands together.

Figure of eight knot – an extra loop creates a larger knot that is more secure when used with calottes.

Bead stitches

There are lots of different ways to stitch beads together to create jewellery and the effects vary depending on the type of bead used. Use a strong thread such as Nymo™ or C-lon™ for best results.

Conditioning thread

Opinions are divided on the use of conditioners such as beeswax and Thread Heaven™. They are specially designed to coat the thread to prevent wear and also prevent knotting and tangling.

Run the thread over the top of the conditioner and then pull the thread between two fingers to distribute the conditioner and create static electricity to prevent tangling.

Using a stop bead

When working some bead stitches, such as peyote stitch, you should secure a bead near the end of the thread to prevent the beads coming off the end.

Pick up a bead on the thread and hold the bead about 10cm (4in) from the end. Take the needle back through the bead twice.

Joining a new thread

Too long a thread can be difficult to handle so you will need to join in a new thread from time to time.

1 Leave the tail and join in a new thread by weaving through the beads, changing direction several times until it comes out the same bead as the old thread.

2 To secure the old thread, weave through several beads and work a half hitch around the core thread. Repeat after a few more beads, sew in the ends and trim.

Right angle weave

In its simple form this stitch is made of units of four beads so that each bead lies at a right angle to the two adjacent beads. The stitch can be worked flat or as a cube. It is one of the easiest bead stitches to work and can be varied by using more beads on each side of the 'square'.

1 Pick up four beads and drop down to the middle of the thread. Form the bead into a ring and pass one end back through the first bead added to create the base unit.

2 From this point on you add three beads only – two beads on one thread and one bead on the other, – carefully passing the single bead thread through the second bead on the other thread.

Making a small cube

1 Make a 3-unit chain in right angle weave. Pick up a bead on each end of the thread and pass the thread back through the bottom bead. Pull the threads to tighten them and the chain will curl up and form into a cube.

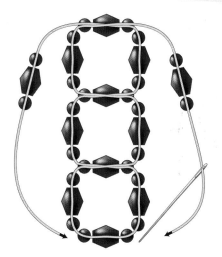

Making a large cube

2 Pick up a seed bead, a large bead and a seed bead and repeat three times. Drop the beads down to the middle of the thread and pass one end back through the first three beads. Follow the diagram to make a 3-unit chain and then add side beads to make the cube as above.

Peyote stitch

This versatile stitch creates a flat bead fabric that can be curved around tubing to create attractive beaded projects. Even number peyote is the simplest peyote technique and suitable for making tubular beads. The first two rows are threaded on to begin and then once the next row is complete the distinctive zigzag pattern makes peyote stitch quite easy to work.

1 Pick up a stop bead (see page 11) and secure about 10cm (4in) from the tail. Pick up the beads required for the first two rows (an even number) and move them down to near the stop bead. To work the third row, pick up one bead and then take the needle through the third bead from the needle.

2 *Pick up a new bead, miss a bead and take the needle through the next bead along. Repeat from * to the end. At the end of this row both the tail and the working thread will come out of the same bead.

3 Once the third row is complete you will have obvious 'up' beads to pass through for subsequent rows. Pick up a bead and pass the needle through the first up bead, continue adding beads to the end of the row. Work the number of rows required.

Making a tube

The flat piece of peyote stitch can be formed into a tube. The zigzag ends butt together neatly and you simply weave between the beads to 'zip' them together.

Top tip

To make a beaded bead roll the peyote panel around a piece of tubing and sew the edges together.

Working with wire

Cutting wire

You can always use strong craft scissors to cut finer wires but it is better to invest in a pair of good quality wire cutters. Look for jewellery tools that are much smaller than tools available in a hardware shop, although heavy-duty cutters are ideal for cutting memory wire, which would damage lightweight tools.

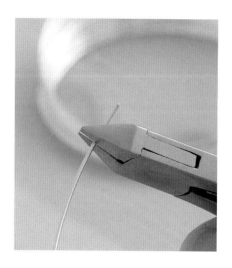

1 Wire cutters have a flat side and an angled side. Cut with the flat side towards the work to get a straight cut on the end of the wire.

2 When cutting a wire that crosses over another wire, use the very tips of the blades to get as close as possible to the crossover point.

Twisting wire

Twist wire to create texture, add body to the wire and make coiling and bending much smoother and kink free.

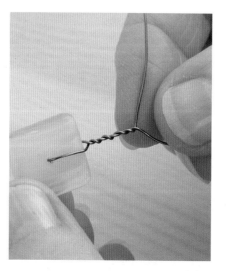

1 Use a bead to give you leverage for twisting the wire. Hold the bead between your finger and thumb and roll it round and round until the wire is evenly twisted along its length.

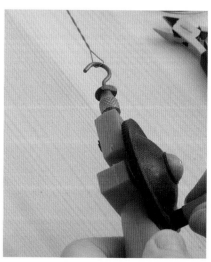

2 A cord maker or hand drill is ideal for twisting lengths of wire. Loop the wire over the hook, secure the ends in a vice and turn the handle to twist. Take care when releasing the wire as it can spring.

Bending wire

Choose flat-nose or snipe-nose pliers to bend wire at an angle. Avoid pliers with a serrated surface that will damage the wire.

1 Hold the wire firmly with the flat-nose pliers so that the edge of the jaw is exactly where you want the wire to bend. Rotate the pliers to create a particular angle.

2 To create a right angle, hold the tail of the wire and push up against the jaws of the pliers with your thumb.

Coiling wire

Coils of wire add a decorative touch to jewellery making. Use round-nose pliers to begin and flat-nose pliers with smooth jaws to coil the wire.

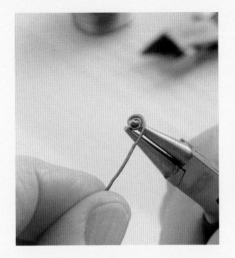

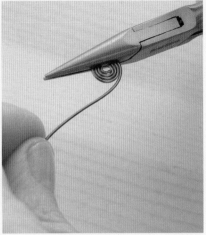

1 To begin the coil, use round-nose pliers to make a small loop at the end of the wire. Hold the wire at the very end of the pliers and bend the wire round. Begin the coiling process by bending the wire around, moving the pliers in the loop.

2 Change to flat-nose pliers and hold the tiny coil flat between the jaws. Bend the wire round against the loop. Keep rotating the coil and bending the wire until it is the size required.

Making a spring

Wrap wire around a mandrel (knitting needle or similar object) to make a tight spring.

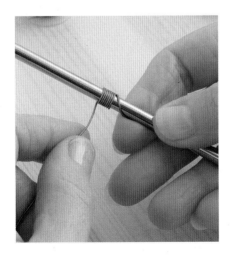

1 Hold the tail of the wire in the palm of your hand and wrap the other end around the mandrel so that the wires fit tightly together.

2 Slide the spring off the mandrel and trim the ends neatly using the flat side of the wire cutters.

Making a bead link

Bead links have a loop at each end of the wire with one or more beads in the middle. They can be joined together to make earrings, bracelets and necklaces. The distance you hold the wire from the top of the round-nose pliers determines the size of the loop. If you use an eyepin to make the link, begin at step 3 or use the plain loop method on page 20.

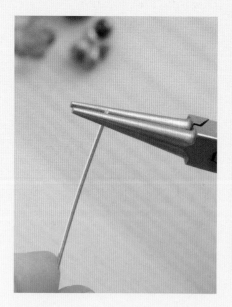

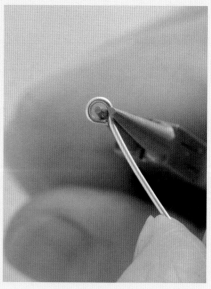

1 To make the first loop, hold the wire about 5mm (³⁄₁₆in) from the end of the round-nose pliers so that the tip of the wire is level with the jaws.

2 Bend the wire around the pliers with your thumb until it touches the tip of the wire. Change the position of the pliers and bend the wire back slightly to straighten the loop.

3 Feed the beads you require onto the end of the wire. Hold the wire in the jaws of the round-nose pliers about 1mm (¹⁄₁₆in) from the beads. Wind the wire around the pliers to make a loop.

4 Cut the wire where it crosses using the very tip of the wire cutters. Hold the ring with flat-nose pliers and bend back to straighten.

Top tip

When winding the wire, pull it away from you, otherwise you may hurt yourself when the pliers slip.

Jump rings

Jump rings are one of the most versatile jewellery findings. They come in a variety of sizes and are normally used to finish off necklaces and bracelets, or to connect charms. Usually round and sometimes oval they should never be pulled apart to open, as the shape will be distorted.

Opening and closing

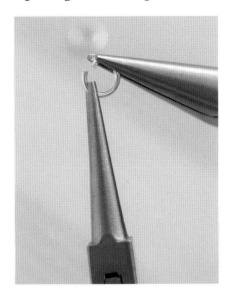
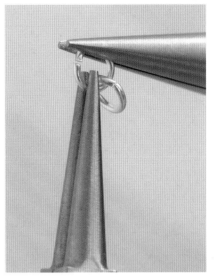

1 Hold the jump ring with two pairs of pliers, either two flat-nose or one with round-nose too. To open the ring, bring one pair of pliers towards you.

2 Attach another ring, chain or jewellery finding. Reverse the action to close, as shown.

Making jump rings

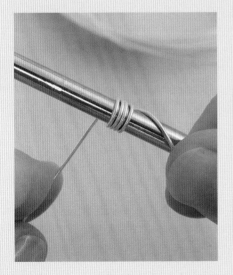

1 Choose a rod of the required diameter – knitting needles are ideal. Hold the end of the wire at one end and wrap tightly around the rod.

2 Slide the closely wound spring off the needle. Use wire cutters to cut each jump ring in turn. Trim the end carefully each time with the flat edge of the wire cutters before cutting the next ring.

3 To tension the jump rings so that they stay closed, push the ends slightly so that they overlap on one side and then the other. Pull back and the ends will spring together.

Making a fishhook fastening

It is quite easy to make your own fastenings with wire. Use wire that is at least 0.7mm (22swg) so that the hook holds its shape in use.

1 Cut the end of the wire with the flat sides of the wire cutters so that it is straight. Hold the wire so that the wire is about 5mm (²⁄₁₀in) from the top of the round-nose pliers and the end of the wire is exactly flush with the edge of the jaws.

2 Using your thumb, bend the wire into a small loop around the jaws of the round-nose pliers. Bend the loop back slightly to staighten.

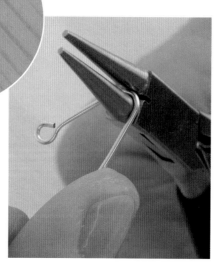

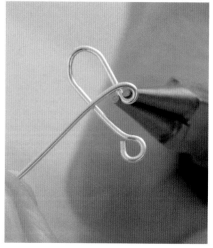

3 Hold the wire about 1.5cm (⅝in) from the loop so that the wire goes across the widest part of the jaws and bend round in the opposite direction.

4 Cut the wire 1cm (½in) from the large bend so that the end is straight. Hold the wire near the tip of the round-nose pliers and bend round to make a tiny loop.

Top tip

Make a large jump ring around the widest part of the round-nose pliers to create the other side of the fastening and attach to the jewellery with small jump rings.

Working with chain

Jewellery chain is available in a variety of styles, materials and quality. Most precious metal chains have soldered links to make the chain much stronger, but many inexpensive chains are not soldered, and so you can open the links with pliers to separate sections if you prefer (see jump rings on page 17).

Cutting chain

Use the tip of your wire cutters to snip into the links.

Measure the length of chain required and then cut through the next link on one side. If the chain is thick or made from hard wire, cut through the other side too so that the link falls away.

Attaching bead charms or jump rings

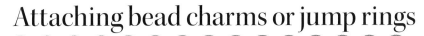

When making a charm bracelet the charms hang better if they are attached to the same side of the chain.

Lay the chain down on the work surface or a beading mat so that it is flat and untwisted. Attach jump rings or charms to the bottom side of alternate links.

Making chain

It is easy to make your own chain using jump rings. You can make more interesting chain by adding two or more links each time.

1 Open one jump ring using two pairs of pliers and pick up two more jump rings. Close the ring using a reverse action.

2 Open further jump rings and add to the end ring until the chain is as long as you require.

Headpins and eyepins

Headpins, which look like large dressmaker's pins, are used to make bead charms that can be hung from bracelets and necklaces or attached to bead links to make earrings. Eyepins are similar but have a large loop at one end.

Top tip

If the headpin goes all the way through the bottom bead, add a small bead first and then the larger bead.

Plain loop

This is an easier way to make a loop on headpins and eyepins as they are made with a harder wire than normal jewellery wire. If the bead slides over the headpin, add a smaller bead such as a seed bead first.

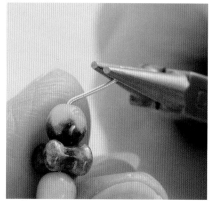

1 Trim the wire to 7mm–1cm (³⁄₁₀in–½in) above the top bead. The distance will depend on the thickness of the wire and the size of the loop required. Make a right angle bend close to the bead.

2 Hold the tip of the wire with round-nose pliers and rotate the pliers to bend the wire part way around the tip.

3 Reposition the pliers and continue rotating the pliers until the tip touches the wire and the loop is in the centre.

Wrapped loop

The wrapped loop is stronger than the plain loop and ideal for beads with slightly larger holes.

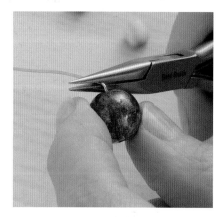

1 You will need at least 3cm (1³⁄₁₀in) of wire above the last bead. Hold the wire above the bead with snipe-nose pliers and bend at a right angle.

2 Hold the wire close to the bend with round-nose pliers and wrap the tail all the way round to form a loop.

3 Hold the loop flat in snipe-nose pliers and wind the wire tail around the stem, covering the gap between the loop and the bead. Trim the tail.

Using filigree caps

These delicate metal caps are available in several sizes to suit different beads and look especially good with pearls. They give a piece of jewellery a more ornate and slightly antique look.

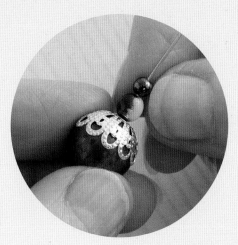

Select the correct size filigree cap to fit the beads you are using. Add the cap at one or both ends of the bead and then continue adding other beads.

Attaching earring wires

Earring wires have a split loop at the bottom that can be opened and closed in a similar way to jump rings.

Hold the earring wire in one hand and the loop with flat-nose pliers. Bring the pliers towards you to open. Attach the earring and reverse the action to close the loop.

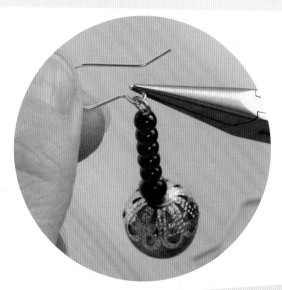

Working with bead sieves

A bead sieve is a piece of mesh or a piece of metal or plastic that has holes punched in it so that you can 'sew' beads on to it. Sieves are usually part of a brooch, pendant or other ready-made jewellery items.

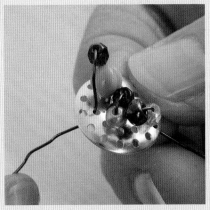

1 You can use the same technique to add beads using thread too. Pick up one or two beads onto wire and feed the ends of the wire through two adjacent holes.

2 Cross the wire at the back and feed one wire up through the holes again. Keep adding beads with one wire and then the other until completely covered. Twist wires at the back to finish.

Working with cords and threads

Nylon filament, tigertail, wax cord, rattail and leather thong are just some of the materials used to string beads for jewellery. Each material has different properties so there are a variety of ways to finish the ends and attach fastenings.

Elastic thread

The easiest way to make a piece of jewellery; use one of two simple techniques to finish.

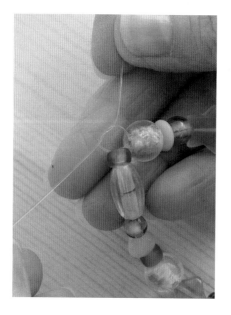

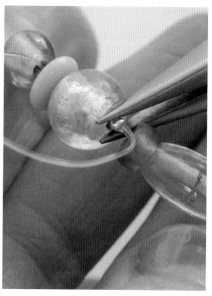

1 Tie the ends of the threads together, working two reef knots (see page 10), one after the other and hide the knot inside a bead with a larger hole.

2 Alternatively, feed the opposite ends through a crimp bead and squeeze to secure. Two crimps spaced a few beads apart is more secure.

Knotting

Knots are used in jewellery making to prevent pearls rubbing together on the string and to space beads along a cord.

1 Pick up a bead on the cord or thread. Tie a loose overhand knot (see page 10).

2 Slip a large needle or 'T' pin into the loop. Manoeuvre the knot along the cord until it is in position and then tighten.

Crimp fastenings

Crimp fastenings come in all shapes and sizes and are used to secure the ends of bead stringing materials so that you can attach jewellery fastenings. Choose the style to suit the material you are using.

Spiral crimp ends

1 Feed the ends of the cord right through the spiral crimp and trim the end.

2 Move the spiral crimp slightly to hide the raw edges and squeeze the end ring only to secure.

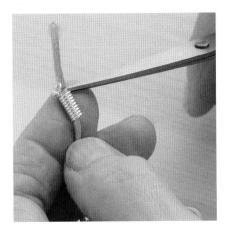
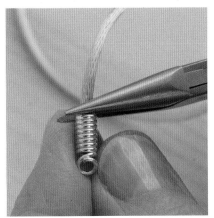

Leather thong ends

Slot the leather thong between the lugs on the fastening and squeeze one side down and then the other to secure.

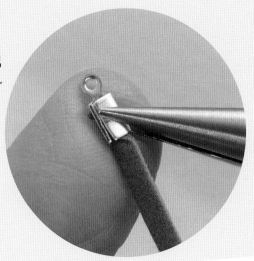

Decorative crimp fastenings

There are lots of different fastenings with a crimp incorporated in the design. These are ideal for finishing wire or tigertail jewellery.

Insert the end of the wire into the fastening. Squeeze the crimp ring with snipe-nose pliers to secure.

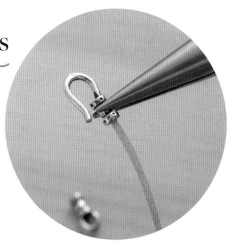

Crimps

Crimps are most often used when stringing with coated wire such as tigertail. They are either tube shaped or round like a doughnut and used to secure beads in position, to create a loop for the clasp or to secure coated wire inside a calotte. You can use flat-nose pliers to secure the crimps or use special crimp pliers for a more professional finish.

Flat-nose pliers

Squeeze the crimp with flat-nose pliers until it is flat. This is usually fairly satisfactory but the edges can be sharp.

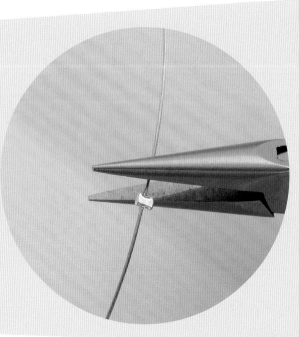

Crimp pliers

Crimp pliers are available in three sizes to suit different sizes of crimp. These have two holes in the jaws, the top one is a plain oval and the one furthest from the tip of the pliers has a dip.

1 Position the crimp in the plain oval and squeeze gently to make it elliptical. Then move the crimp to the oval with the dip and squeeze to make the crimp curl.

2 Move the crimp to the plain oval and turn so that it is vertical then squeeze the pliers to compress the crimp into a rounded shape.

Spacing beads with crimps

Tigertail, softflex and other coated wires can't be knotted and so the beads are spaced out using crimps.

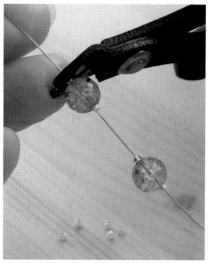

1 Feed the beads onto the wire with a crimp at either end. Secure the first crimp onto the wire using flat-nosed pliers or crimp pliers.

2 Hold the wire up so that the beads and second crimp drop down to sit against the secured crimp. Squeeze the second crimp in position.

Attaching clasps with a crimp

Use this secure method to create a loop at the end of a piece of jewellery.

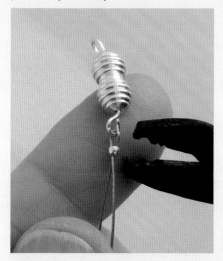

1 Thread the crimp onto the wire, pick up a jump ring or fastening and feed the tail back through the crimp to create a loop. Compress the crimp so it sits 1–2mm (1⁄16–1⁄10in) from the jump ring or fastening.

2 Continue stringing beads. At the other end pick up a crimp bead and the jump ring or fastening. Feed the tail back through the crimp and a few beads. Compress the crimp as before and trim the tail between the beads.

Top tip

Use crimp beads with stiff kinds of bead cord like tigertail and monofilament.

Knot covers

Calottes, or clamshells, are similar small knot covers used to cover the raw ends of thread, wire of fine ribbon when stringing beads. The clamshell, shown here, has a hole on the hinge. A calotte has the hole at one side and you simply lay the knotted bead in the slot then close with pliers.

Cord or ribbon

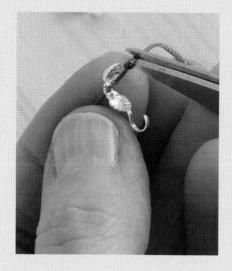 

1 Feed the open calotte onto the thread or cord and tie a knot. Trim the end close to the knot.

2 Bring the calotte down so that it covers the knot. Close the calotte with pliers.

Tigertail

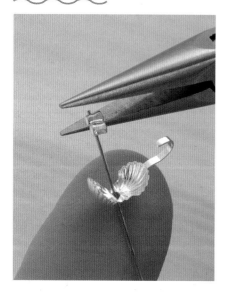 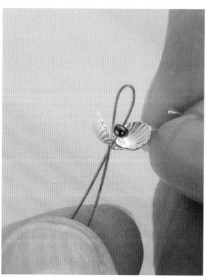 

1 When using tigertail or other coated wires that don't knot easily secure the end of the wire with one or two crimps and then close the calotte to hide the crimp, as shown.

2 Alternatively, pick up a clamshell and a seed bead. Take the tail back through the clamshell.

3 Pick up two or three beads and a crimp. Pull wire taut. Squeeze the crimp bead and trim the end. Close the calotte with pliers.

End caps

These decorative findings, usually tulip- or cone-shaped, are used to cover crimps or knots at the end of necklaces or bracelets. There are several techniques that can be used to secure the threads, so choose one to suit the material you are using and a style and size of end cap that will completely hide any knots or raw ends.

Tigertail

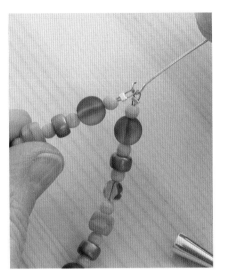
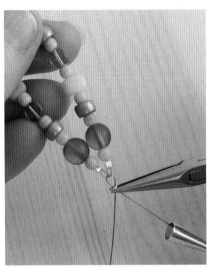

1 Finish multistrand tigertail necklaces by making a loop with crimps on the end of each strand. Attach the loops onto an eyepin and feed the end through the end cap.

2 If you are planning to go from a multistrand to a single strand on a necklace make a crimp loop on a length of tigertail and thread through the multistrands, as pictured.

Cord or ribbon

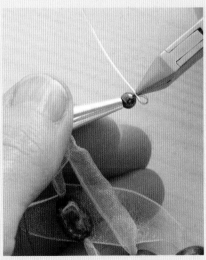

1 With cord or ribbon, tie a large overhand knot at the end. Wrap craft wire around the knot, leaving a tail out the top. For added security apply a little beading glue into the knot before adding the end cap.

2 Add a small bead to reduce the hole size at the top of the end cap. Use round-nose pliers to make a loop on the end of the wire and attach the clasp of your choice.

Super Sparkle

Sparkle & Shine

Make sure you dazzle this summer with this glitzy crystal jewellery. These stunning items are easy to create and guaranteed to catch everyone's eye. They might not be diamonds, but these Swarovski crystals produce the most beautiful flashes of light, with the added bonus of being available in a brilliant range of colours. Using a two needle, right angle weave technique, we've made bands of beading and crystal cubes then threaded them onto red wire for fantastic looking designs in hot, spicy shades.

YOU WILL NEED:

- Beads: crystals, Swarovski, bicone, 4mm (³⁄₁₆in), fire opal, siam, light siam; round, clear, 8mm (³⁄₈in); spacer, vermeil, 22 carat gold; seed, size 11; crimps, gold
- Thread, beading
- Needles, two, size 12
- Calotte ends, gold
- Fastener, toggle, gold
- Wire, beading, flexible, 0.18mm (34swg), red
- Scissors
- Pliers, flat-nose

Earrings:
- Headpins, gold
- Earrings, fish hook, pair, gold
- Pliers, round-nose

Designer
Gillian Slone

Orange Necklace

1 To make a small cube, attach a needle to each end of 60cm (24in) of thread, and string on four bicone crystals. Centre them, and lay on a flat surface with a needle either side. Pass the right one through the first crystal after the left needle (see step 1 diagram for right angle weave on page 12), ensuring it doesn't pierce the cotton.

2 The two needles will swap sides with the right becoming the left and vice versa. In their new positions, pull them away from each other to create the cube's first side. String two bicones to the left needle and one to the right (*). Lay the weaving flat. As before, run the right needle through the crystal immediately after the left needle (see step 2 on page 12). Changing places again, pull them apart to form the second side. Repeat once more from (*).

3 String one bicone to each needle. Lay the work flat. Pass right needle horizontally through the bottom crystal of the strip of weaving, from right to left (see diagram for making a small cube on page 12). Leave the thread slack for now. Repeat passing the left needle into the base crystal, this time left to right.

4 Slowly pull both needles away from each other to cause the gems to curl into a cube. Ensure the thread doesn't wrap around the beads. If it does, loosen until the weaving is flat then start the process again.

5 Weave one needle through the crystals to meet up with the other. Tension the threads to remove any gaps, then knot the ends together. Tie again in the same place. Reinforce the cube by passing each needle in turn through a few beads,

then tighten around the existing thread. Repeat several times, all around the shape. Knot and trim tail threads. Make three more.

6 For the large cube, apply the same technique, but in place of each crystal use a bicone sandwiched between two size 11 seed beads (see diagram for making a large cube, page 12). Close the design by passing through the bottom three sparklers comprised of a seed, crystal, and another seed bead. Gently push a round crystal through one side into the centre. Re-tension to encase the large gem. Reinforce, knot and secure.

7 To assemble, cut two 40cm (16in) lengths of flexible wire. Pass both together through a crimp, two or three gold spacer beads and the large cube. Add further spacers and a crimp. Adjust so 3–5cm (1–2in) extends

Top tip

When spacing beads with crimps, always check that the crimps are quite secure before moving on to the next.

Once you've got the hand of this technique there's no stopping what you can create!

Red Necklace | Earrings

from one side of the beads with the lengths slightly staggered. Using pliers, flatten crimps close to the gems to hold in place.

8 On one wire, string the small cubes with a bicone and crimp either side, alternating with single crystals between two crimps and flatten to hold in place. Repeat for the second length. Fix single crystals in place on the short protruding wires.

9 Thread a crimp, crystal, calotte and one seed to one end of the wire. Pass back through all, but the seed bead. Do the same at the other side. Flatten the crimps and trim any excess. Close the calottes over the seeds, and slip the clasp onto the hooks. Use pliers to close.

Weave bicone crystals as for the small cubes, but omit the final single beads to each thread, and leave flat. Weave back through the gems, keeping a tight tension and knot in several places. Work three strips, one longer than the others. String onto the wire with single crystals and gold spacers in between the strips. Add a clasp as before.

String bicone and spacer beads onto a headpin and cut the excess to 1cm (½in). Using pliers, make a right angle bend after the last gem. Hold the tip with round-nose pliers and roll into a loop. String a second headpin with fewer sparklers. Open the eye on the fish hook earring, drop both pieces inside and close up.

Bracelet

On two separate lengths of wire, fix small cubes and bicones in position. Feed both pieces together through a crimp, bicone, crimp, calotte, and another crimp. Adjust to the required length, then flatten the crimps to fix. The last one should sit inside the calotte. Trim the excess and add a fastener.

Top tip

Condition your thread with a wax, such as Thread Heaven™, when working right angle weaves to stop the gems from slipping.

Heart's Desire

This design may look intricate but is very easy to do, even if you are new to working with wire. With the correct materials romantic heart shapes can be created in minutes, adorned with glittering beads and presented on a sumptuous velvet card. Handmade gifts are always more touching, so get to work on this pretty set and show how much you really care. Why not make up the matching earrings as a little treat to yourself? Go on, spread a little love!

YOU WILL NEED:

- Silver wire: 0.6mm (23swg), 51cm (20in); 0.4mm (27swg), 2m (79in)
- Seed beads, size 10, 5g (0.17oz)
- Swarovski bicone crystals, assorted 3mm (⅛in), 4mm (³⁄₁₆in), 5mm (²⁄₁₀in), 25
- Earring wires, silver, two
- Card blank
- Powder, silver
- Velvet, 10cm (4in) square
- Envelope

Tools:
- Wire cutters
- Round-nose pliers
- Flat-nose pliers
- Hot glue gun
- Pinking shears

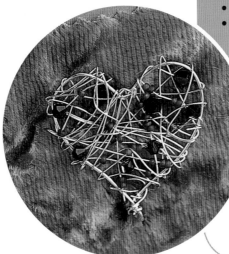

Designer
Jema Hewitt

Earrings

1 To make the earrings, firstly, put aside two matching 5mm (⅛in) bicones and two sets of 4mm (⅛in) for the earring stems. Cut two 13cm (5in) lengths of 0.6mm (23swg) wire. Holding one piece about 2.5cm (1in) from the end with the flat-nose pliers, make a sharp bend. Use both round-nose and flat-nose pliers to carefully shape it into a heart, as shown. You should end up where you started, at the bottom point.

2 Two pieces of wire should now cross each other at the base of the heart, as shown. Hold the longer piece of wire in a pair of pliers and then carefully twist the first one around it a few times to secure the shape. Trim the short end with a pair of cutters but leave the longer one as it is. This will eventually form the stem to attach the earring wire to.

3 Cut a 38cm (15in) length of 0.4mm (27swg) wire. Secure it at the base of the heart frame and wind it tightly around the thicker one a couple of times. Thread on a colour co-ordinated selection of seed beads and crystals in the order you prefer, as shown. Then start to spiral the thin wire around the shape, making sure each loop is tight. Wind up and down as well as around, densely covering the frame for mesh effect.

4 If you find that the wire is starting to slip and seems to be going over the same section, weave the wire through as well as around. Filter the beads along a few at a time, as shown, so that there are a few dotted all over the heart. Decide at the beginning which side is the front and position all the beads on that side. Wrap round the thicker wire and trim with wire cutters.

5 Take the long stem of wire and bend it up behind the back of the heart, pushing it forward between the dip at the top. Use round-nose pliers to make a right-angle bend to send it upwards once more, as this will help the earring to hang straight. Thread on one crystal from each matching pair that you set aside at the beginning.

6 To create the top loop, grip the round-nose pliers 2.5cm (1in) from the top of the wire. Twist them through 90°, away from you, creating a right angle. With your free hand curve the top piece back towards you, shaping it tightly over the top of the pliers. Slide the cutters inside the loop and carefully snip. Open the earring wires loop by twisting, and thread on the pendant. Finally, twist again to close. The pair of earrings are now ready to be worn.

Top tip

Alternatively, make a pendant to hang from a ready-made chain. Or twist a larger heart shape and attach a pin at the back for an attractive brooch.

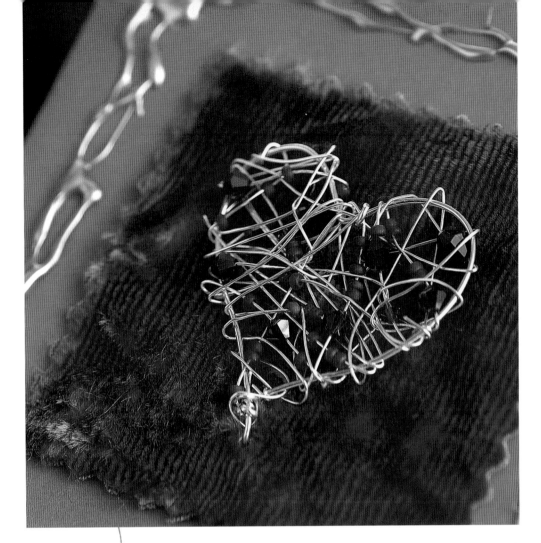

Card

1 Using pinking shears, trim a piece of velvet into a square, big enough that so that you can see an edging around it when the heart shape is stuck on top, and stick to the card. You can use a shop-bought card blank or create one yourself by deciding on the shape and dimensions that would best suit the design and then cutting a piece of card to fit.

2 Use a glue gun to create random scribbles and swirls in a border. Keeping the gun moving all the time, make any interesting pattern of your choice. Once the glue is completely dry, put a small amount of metal powder on a large soft brush and carefully dust across the glue pattern created. Cover the shapes thoroughly with the metal and blow away any of the powder excess.

3 To make the heart, cut 26cm (10in) of 0.6mm (23swg) wire and continue in the same way as you did for the earrings, but this time stop after completing step four. Use the remaining crystals and seed beads and carefully squeeze the wire between your fingers to flatten the weave for a more visual effect.

4 Carefully make an incision in the card and velvet with a bradawl where the point of the heart will be, and then another incision at the centre of the heart. Then thread the stem through the bottom and back out of the top. Trim the end to finish the card. A matching gift-tag and colour co-ordinating bag or tissue paper would finish it off and make it an extra special gift.

Basic equipment, including round-nose and flat-nose pliers and wire cutters, works wonders in creating this pretty set

Top tip

Practice glue designs on scrap card before applying to the velvet.

Perfect Timing

Create beautiful jewellery pieces that are too good to cover up and be ahead of the fashion crowd with one of these stunning creations. Made with Swarovski crystal beads and pearls, the bag charm is very now, and with the added bonus of a watch, it serves a purpose too! Just place units of gems onto pins and you'll never be late again, looking chic and stylish in the bargain. If you're taken by the striking bracelet design, it may be surprising to hear that it's actually very easy to make. Simply thread your chosen sparklers on wire to create something truly individual.

Designer
Atelier Rayher

Watch Charm

1 For the base of each chain, thread beads or charms of your choice onto jewellery pins, and bend the top of the wire around the tips of round-nose pliers, creating a link. Using chain stitch pins, make up several units of gems, and fix them together by carefully opening and closing the ends. Vary the lengths of each 'string', for added interest.

2 Add the watch face, by attaching it to a row of three chain link pins. Decorate the bottom with a blossom charm, antique anchor chain, and a bead unit. Make a long 'string' from antique anchor chain. Embellish by adding pearls and glass beads along the length. Attach a ring to each piece, and hook onto the key holder. Finish with a glass heart. This can then be clipped to a bag using the snap-hook, to finish.

If you've never thought of using your beading skills to create a watch strap, these sparkling designs are sure to inspire

YOU WILL NEED:

Watch Charm:
- Beads: polished, crystal, Swarovski, 4mm (³⁄₁₆in), cardinal red, pink chiffon; 6mm (¼in), pink chiffon; crystal X dice, moonstone; glass, renaissance, 4mm (³⁄₁₆in), 6mm (¼in), pale pink, orchid; pearls; heart, glass, brick red
- Charms, blossom, antique rose
- Key holder, with snap-hook
- Pins: chain stitch, platinum, 5cm (2in); jewellery, platinum, 4cm (1.5in)
- Anchor chain, antique, oxidized silver, 1.2mm (18swg)
- Cap, filigree, platinum, 7mm (³⁄₁₀in)
- Rings, antique, oxidized silver, 7mm (³⁄₁₀in)
- Antique jewellery, part no. 2, oxidized silver
- Watch, jewellery, white

Tools:
- Pliers, round-nose

Bracelet Watch:
- Beads: polished, crystal, Swarovski, 6mm (¼in), classic red, midnight blue, jade, coral red, olive, ice blue
- Watch, jewellery, blue
- Wire, jewellery, 0.4mm (27swg)
- Spring hook, antique, oxidized silver
- Rings, antique, oxidized silver, 7mm (³⁄₁₀in)
- Crimps, 1.8mm (¹⁄₁₀in), platinum

Tools:
- Pliers, flat-nose

Bracelet Watch

1 Pass wire through each eye of a jewellery watch so that there are two strings on both sides of the face. Thread on crystal beads, following the picture. Start with two gems, one per length, and then cross through a third. Continue until you've reached the ideal size for your wrist.

2 Fix an antique ring on one end, and a spring hook to the other. Secure each end of the wire through the findings with a crimp. To fasten, squeeze with flat-nose pliers, and trim the excess.

Mint Finish

Add instant glamour to your summer finery and accessorise with these dazzling silver-plated pieces. It's so trendy to create and personalise chic designer-style jewellery, but with so many beads and accessories to choose from it's sometimes difficult to know where and when to begin. For this project we started with silver-plated, mesh setting blanks and added some gorgeous crystals and pretty beads to create a stunning bracelet and pendant. The mesh setting holds all the sparkly bits firmly in position.

Top tip

Discover a wealth of products to choose from in your local craft shop, including equipment and beads.

Designer
EFCO Hobbies

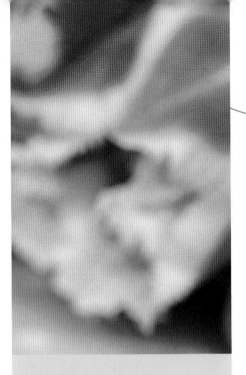

Heart Pendant

1 Remove the mesh sieve in the middle of the blank pendant. String six Indian beads onto the thread and sew into the middle. Secure beads by over-sewing the back of the sieve several times.

2 Sew on eight 6mm (¼in) fuchsia crystals onto the sieve. To finish off the design, continue adding 35 of the Indian beads around the edge of the mesh. Once the entire surface is completely covered, over-sew the back to secure.

3 Cover the entire jewellery base with glue and gently push the sieve into place. Hold in place until secure. Again using the adhesive, stick the flatstone beads around the outer edge of the heart pendant.

YOU WILL NEED:
- Arm bangle, silver-plated with magnetic clasp
- Pendant, heart, silver-plated
- Beads: Indian, silver-lined, mauve; Swarovski crystals, 6mm (¼in), 4mm (³⁄₁₆in), fuchsia; crystal flatstone, fuchsia
- Thread, beading, fine
- Needle, beading
- Glue, DekoFix

Use your favourite beads to create a stylish fashion accessory

Bracelet

1 Remove one of the sieves from the bracelet. String six Indian beads onto the beading thread and sew into the middle of the sieve. Secure these by over-sewing the back of the sieve several times.

2 Sew six of the 4mm (³⁄₁₆in) fuchsia crystals onto the mesh sieve, as shown (left). Add 30 Indian beads around the edge of the metal to complete the design. Once the entire surface is covered and you are happy that there are no gaps, over-sew the back to secure.

3 Using glue, cover the entire jewellery base and gently push the beaded sieve into place. Hold for several moments to make sure that it is secure. To finish, repeat this process for the four remaining mesh discs on the bracelet.

Top tip

This lovely heart pendant comes with its own narrow leather necklace and silver clasp.

Iced Gems

Create a stunning piece of jewellery using only three tools. These attractive bead baubles are not only fun to make but look distinctive and striking for parties and evenings out. You could also suspend the clusters from nylon cord or organza ribbons to adorn a window. Watch as the light catches and reflects off the crystal facets. Alternatively, attach to a key ring or turn it into a trendy handbag charm. These ideas can be easily tailored to your own specifications by altering the size of the beads and varying the colour combinations. It's a great way of using up gems you may already have, and once you've created one, we're sure you'll be hooked!

YOU WILL NEED:

- Wire, silver, 0.8mm (21swg)
- Nylon filament/fishing line, clear, 0.5mm (25swg)
- Crimps, silver, 1mm (19swg) diameter
- Assorted beads, 10mm (½in), 6mm (¼in), 4mm (³⁄₁₆in)
- Chain, silver
- Cotton cord, black, 1mm (19swg)
  - Ear wires

Tools:
  - Pliers: round-nose; flat-nose
  - Wire cutters

Designer
Linda Jones

Cord Necklace

1 To start the necklace, thread your beads onto the wire – you should be able to fit two or three on each piece. Use the smaller styles to plug the ends of the larger ones, for a neat finish. With the tips of a pair of round-nose pliers, form a little hook at the end of the wire. Carefully squeeze this together with a pair of flat-nose pliers to make a stopper, or headpin.

2 Next, cut the wire off the spool, making sure to leave a length of 1.5cm (⅝in) extending from the bead hole on the opposite side of the headpin. Fold the wire to a right angle, using the tips of a pair of round-nose pliers. To form a link, hold the end of this wire firmly in the pliers and push slightly down before carefully curling around until it meets. See page 16 for further instructions on making a bead link.

3 Continue threading the varied beads, until you have created fourteen units. To make the necklace 'tassel', cut several different lengths of silver chain – each should be very slightly longer than the other. Alternatively, you can use pieces of 0.8mm (21swg) silver wire. Now form small headpins at the ends, as you did before.

4 Thread on the small beads you wish to suspend onto the wires. Now make links at the top, as you did before, by initially bending the wire 90º and then moulding it around a pair of round-nose pliers to form a circular loop.

5 Cut 10cm (4in) of clear nylon filament and thread the units onto this, positioning the wire rods or chains that will form the central tassel in the middle. Slide a silver crimp onto the ends of

the nylon, bringing the beads together to form the bauble shape. Squeeze the crimp tightly to secure.

6 Cut off one of the projecting ends of nylon and thread your top bead onto the remaining extending filament. Slide on another silver crimp and curl the nylon into a loop, slotting it back into the crimp. Squeeze tightly to secure. Align the bauble so that the beads sit in a balanced fashion and the tassel is suspended from the centre.

Colour co-ordinate the beads to match your bag, shoes or dress for a totally matching outfit from head to toe

Top tip

To strengthen the coils, harden by hammering gently on a steel block.

44

Bead Bauble

1 Make another bauble up in the same way as for the cord necklace design, using cornflower blue and cerise beads instead. Instead of using headpins at the end of each unit however, this time create spirals, as shown. If you want to make a closed coil, then begin with a headpin.

2 Then, grip the end of the wire very tightly in a pair of flat-nose pliers and begin carefully winding the wire around itself. Make sure to keep curling continuously, using your fingers to guide it.

3 Keep going until you are completely satisfied with the shape that you have created. Then cut the wire off the spool, making sure that you leave enough wire to add the beads and fashion a link to finish the bead bauble.

Have fun by experimenting with a mixture of subtle shaded beads of all shapes and sizes, and come up with something totally unique!

Earrings

1 A pair of matching earrings would finish off the necklace perfectly. To create this beautiful pair, first complete a smaller bauble in the same way as before. Use the same colours as the necklace for an exact matching set, or else use co-ordinating shades for a different look.

2 When you are happy with the size of the bauble, then insert the nylon filament into ear wires. Close up with a crimp as before.

Top tip

Try using these dazzling clusters to add sparkle to a whole number of projects, from necklaces to decorative bag charms.

Bead Dazzle

No need to trawl the high street for that perfect trinket to match your outfit – this project shows how easy it can be to make your own. This jewellery looks so gorgeous it's hard to believe you could make it yourself, but once you've got the hang of stringing components together using pliers, headpins and jump rings there'll be no stopping you! Don't be put off by the terminology: jump rings are small hoops of wire that can be opened and closed to form links, while headpins are literally pin-shaped wires with a stopper on one end; thread on your beads to make drops for necklaces and earrings and then bend the top to create a link. The only vital tools are two pairs of jewellery pliers to grip the components with – arm yourself with these and away you go!

YOU WILL NEED:

Silver necklace:
- Leather-like cord, square, pink; metal ornament; beads, metal, small; ring and bar clasp, large; end cap; jump rings 1 x 4mm (³/₁₆in)

Pink cord necklace and bracelet:
- Leather-like cord, square, pink; ring and bar clasp, large; glass beads, assorted sets: pink, green; faceted glass beads, pale green; faceted beads, diamond, crystal amethyst; jump rings, 1 x 4mm (³/₁₆in); end cap; headpin, silver

Heart necklace and bracelet:
- Leather-like cord, square, pink; pendant, platinum heart; jump rings, 1 x 4mm (³/₁₆in); end caps; bolt rings, silver

Ring and earrings:
- Ring, adjustable, silver; headpin, silver, 30mm (1¹/₅in); jump rings, 1 x 4mm (³/₁₆in); faceted beads, diamond, crystal amethyst; ear wires, rings, silver; bison power glue

Tools:
- Jewellery pliers, round-nose, two pairs

Designer
Amanda Walker

47

Silver necklace

1 Cut a length of pink cord 38cm (15in) long or whatever length will fit comfortably around your neck. Thread on a small metal bead and, using the pliers, encase the end of the cord with an end cap.

2 From the other end of the cord thread a long larger bead and then a small metal bead. As before, thread on a small metal bead and then end-cap the remaining end of the cord. Carefully trim away any excess cord.

3 Using a pair of pliers, open a jump ring. Next, onto it carefully thread the eye of the end cap and the ring of the clasp. Close the ring. Then repeat to the other end of the necklace, attaching the bar of the clasp, to finish the necklace.

Pink cord necklace and bracelet

1 To make this striking cord necklace and bracelet, shown at the top of the next page, firstly cut lengths of cord 88cm (35in) long for the necklace and 36cm (14in) for the bracelet. Next, thread the bar of the clasp onto the shorter piece of cord and double it back on itself. Then, onto this double cord, thread a small metal bead – this will secure the bar (you may need to use a large sewing needle to achieve this process).

2 Attach an end cap to the other end, then a jump ring with the ring of the clasp attached to it. Close the ring.

3 Thread three headpins with crystal amethyst beads and then a combination of the other larger beads, placing a crystal in between each of these beads and finishing with a crystal. Using the pliers, bend the end of the pin over to form a ring.

4 Open a jump ring and thread on three beaded pins, and then attach this to the bar of the clasp. Repeat this process with the longer piece of cord to make the necklace.

Top tip

Make it easier to pick up tiny beads and thin wires by keeping a pair of fine tweezers to hand.

These pieces would make a perfect gift for a treasured friend, simply wrap in colour co-ordinated tissue paper and make a matching card

Heart necklace and bracelet

1 For the necklace, cut a 44cm (17½in) piece of pink cord and for the bracelet an 18cm (7in) piece. Attach end caps to all the ends, then jump rings, then bolt rings. Open two jump rings and thread on the platinum hearts. Close the rings around the cords of the necklace and bracelet.

Ring and Earrings

1 For the ring, thread a headpin through a metal bead and, using the pliers, bend the point of the pin into a ring. This needs to be sitting right on top of the hole of the bead; to achieve this you may need to cut off a little of the pin with the pliers.

2 Thread ten headpins with crystal amethysts. Cut off the end of the pin leaving enough to bend into a ring (approximately 1cm (⅜in)). Open a jump ring and thread on all the crystals. Attach the jump ring to the ring on top of the metal bead. Using the glue, stick the metal bead to the flat disc on top of the ring.

3 To make the earrings, assemble six headpins with crystals for each one, attach these to a jump ring and the jump ring to the earring.

Crown Jewels

Become a princess with a beautiful pink and purple headpiece. What a gorgeous accessory for a wedding or special event! This tiara has a delicate open weave to complement all those beautiful lacy gowns so popular this spring. The latticed effect of the woven wire components perfectly combine with the rose petal pink beads and crystals, just like flowers growing up a trellis. What's more, it's very simple to make, so you too can be the belle of the ball this summer.

Top tip

Always check the size of the holes through your beads – some can be too narrow to fit through certain gauges of wire.

Designer
Jema Hewitt

Beaded Tiara

YOU WILL NEED:

- Silver tiara band
- Pearls, natural 'rice crispy', 25, dyed pink
- Stone chips, semi precious, 25
- Crystals, bicone: 5mm (⅕in) blush pink, 15; 4mm (³⁄₁₆in), ice pink, 15
- Wire, silver-plated, 4m (13ft) x 0.4mm (27swg)

Tools

- Wire cutters
- Chain or flat-nose pliers

1 Cut 20, 19cm (7½in) lengths of 0.4mm (27swg) wire and 10, 16mm (⅗in) pieces. To make the first wire strand component, thread a 5mm (⅕in) crystal onto a 19cm (7½in) wire and push down to halfway. Hold the crystal in one hand and bend the wire in half with the other. Continue holding the gem in one hand and place your thumb and finger of the other hand one the wires on the other side, close to the crystal.

2 Start turning the crystal gently but firmly so the wires below it twist together. Guide your fingers down the wires for about an inch and continue to turn the gem four or five times until you have created a nice tight texture. Don't over-twist or you will break it. Thread a pearl onto just one of the wire ends, hold the bead in one hand and continue to twist as before, for about an inch.

3 Thread on a stone chip and twist as before all the way down to the bottom. Make up the rest of the components in the same way, varying the order, colour and sizes of the beads you thread on. Continue down to the bottom. Thread the shorter wire lengths with just two gems. As you work, place the wires out in front of you with the longer ones in the centre, gradually getting shorter at the sides, to check the arrangement as you go.

4 Place them on a dark piece of foam for best visibility. Take alternate wires and slant them to the right then slant the remaining pieces to the left. Rearrange until happy with the way the pieces interact together. Make up more components if you want, or slightly longer ones – each tiara should be unique so experiment.

5 When you are happy with the final arrangement, straighten up all the wires once more, then use the chain-nose pliers to bend a right angle, 5cm (2in) from the bottom of each wire. The 15 wires that will be on the right side need to bend to the right and the 15 on the left should bend to the left. Cut about 40cm (16in) of the 0.4mm (27swg) wire. Hold the bent section of the right middle wire along the inside edge of the tiara band. Position it slightly right of centre and, using the 0.4mm (27swg) wire, secure it tightly for about 1cm (½in).

6 Add the next component on the right in the same way and continue wrapping tightly with the 0.4mm (27swg) wire, catching both bent sections behind the band. Keep adding components at 0.5cm (⅕in) intervals until one side is complete, then go back to the middle with a new piece of 0.4mm (27swg) wire and do the other side. Use only the minimum amount of wrapping necessary to make it really secure – too much gets bulky.

7 Once all the pieces are firmly attached bend alternate components to the right and the remaining wires to the left. Starting at the centrepiece, weave the wire loosely under and over the wires that cross it then move to the next wire that the component crossed over. Continue with all the pieces until you have a nice firm mesh, rearrange to make sure you are perfectly happy.

Top tip

For a stunning compact version of the tiara, opt for slightly shorter wires with the beads spaced closer together.

Funky Beads

More Gems

Create stunning bead-encrusted jewellery for high glamour. Whether it's sophisticated elegance or frivolous extravagance you're looking for, we've got just the necklace. We have weaved tiny beads into strips using even count flat peyote stitch and wrapped it around a tubular support to create dazzling embellishments. Beads with an iris or metallic finish reflect the light beautifully and are ideal for plain weaving. If you fancy something even more elaborate, make up some of these fab caterpillar focal points that form the basis of the second design. You'll be spoilt for choice!

YOU WILL NEED:

Elegant:
- Beads: delica; round metal, 2.4mm (1/10in), 6.5mm (3/10in), seed, size 11, assorted decorative
- Clear plastic tube, 6mm (1/4in) exterior diameter
- Beading thread, grade D
- Needle, Sharps, size 12
- Bead wire
- Crimps and toggle fastener

Extravagant:
As above, plus:
- Beads: seed, size 6, size 8; bugle, 3mm (1/10in)

Tools:
- Scissors
- Pliers

Designer
Gillian Slone

Elegant

1 Thread a needle with a metre of cotton. Position a delica bead 10cm (4in) from the end, go through it twice more in the same direction, creating a stopper. Pick up 12 gems for rows one and two (six beads each row). For row three, string a gem (A on diagram for step 1, page 13), reverse the direction and pass through the second to last delica (B on diagram for step 1, page 13) of the initial 12.

2 Add a delica and run through the next but one bead (C). Repeat along the row, keeping the tension firm. Finish by passing through the first strung bead (D on diagram for step 2, page 13). Remove stopper. For the fourth and subsequent rows, pick up a gem (E on diagram for step 2, page 13), change direction and pass through the first prominent bead on the previous row (F).

3 Pull the thread firmly to lock the edge bead in position. Add a delica (G on diagram for step 1, page 13) and pass through the next proud bead (H). Continue, attaching six gems in all. For row five, string a bead, turn and repeat as for row four. Keep adding until the weaving is long enough for the jagged ends to interlock when wrapped around plastic tubing. We worked 28 rows (counting diagonally).

4 To finish off any short thread, weave diagonally through several beads and rows, doubling back occasionally. Secure new lengths the same way. Join the ends. Next, emerge from a final edge bead and pass down the corresponding gem at the other end of the strip. The zigzag ends should butt together neatly (see diagram for making a tube, page 13).

5 Zig-zag between the beads to zip the ends together, finish off and snip the tails. Cut plastic tubing the same length as the beading and slide into the centre. Secure a 30cm (12in) length of thread. Emerge from an edge delica, pick up a 2.4mm (¹⁄₁₀in) metal bead and pass down adjacent bead. Pass up the next edge delica, string a metal gem and go down the following delica.

6 Add a third metal bead, but this time pass down the previous delica. Change direction again, exit a delica and add a metal gem. Repeat, with 10 or 11 metal beads in all. Pass into the nearest metal bead and run the thread through each metal gem in turn. Thread into the delicas and secure. Repeat at the other end of the tube. Make three more in the same way.

Top tip

As an alternative, use just one embellished bead in your necklace to create a stunning focal point.

Make this jewellery the focal point of your outfit by combining it with plain dark colours such as a black wrap dress

Extravagant

7 Create the central bead using eight gems each row (initially stringing 16 beads for rows one and two). To embellish, emerge from a bead six in from the edge, counting on the diagonal (W on diagram 1, page 118). String a delica, small metal bead, then a delica. Pass diagonally over four beads and into the sixth in from the opposite edge (X).

8 Weave into the next bead (Y), string embellishment and pass into gem next to the first you emerged from (Z). Repeat around the tube and secure. Cut wire 10cm (4in) longer than final length required. Add crimp and toggle to one end, pass tail back through and close with pliers. Trim excess, then thread seed and other gems onto wire by hand, without a needle. Add beaded tubes between two 6.5mm (³⁄₁₀in) metal beads. Crimp with other toggle part.

1 For the green caterpillars, weave a strip as before, but work only 14 rows. Join the jagged ends, omitting the tube support and metal beads around the edges. Emerge from any bead of the tube (A on diagram 2, page 118, Useful Diagrams), pick up one size 8 seed, a size 11 and a delica. Skip the delica and go back down the seeds. Pass into a nearby bead. (B) Tension the thread firmly to pull the embellishment tight. Repeat randomly to cover completely.

2 The burgundy caterpillars are made using size 6 seed beads with the weaving of the central piece nine gems wide. Make shorter ones (four per row) for the light green tube. Embellish as for the central tube bead of the 'Elegant' necklace. Decorate the short burgundy design with a single row of caterpillar style embellishment. For the dark green designs, use four delicas and replace the small metal gems with bugle beads, adjusting the spacing as necessary.

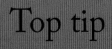

Top tip

To weave more rows, use larger diameter plastic tubing which can be bought from DIY stores.

Razzle Dazzle

Transform a handful of humble safety pins into a super-stylish beaded bracelet. Fashionable accessory stores are brimming with bright, ethnic and boho style beads this autumn, made into unique garments, bags, necklaces and bangles. These unusual blue and green toned stretchy bracelets are inspired by those produced in South African townships where the skilled women designers continue a long tradition of decorative glass beadwork.

Top tip

Choose toning beads for a sophisticated bracelet, or contrasting colours for a more funky look.

Designer
Lucinda Ganderton

YOU WILL NEED:

Blue Bracelet:
- Safety pins, 3cm (1⅕in), 28
- Beads: glass, 15mm (⁶⁄₁₀in) rectangular, blue; 4mm (³⁄₁₆in) iridescent, green, 72; 5mm (⅕in)

Green Bracelet:
- Safety pins, 2.5cm (1in), 34
- Beads: glass, 5mm (⅕in), matte turquoise, 68; 4mm (³⁄₁₆in), clear green, 51; 3mm (¹⁄₁₀in), clear green, 68; 6mm (¼in) faceted amber, 17; 4mm (³⁄₁₆in) iridescent green, 68

Tools:
- Bead elastic, clear
- Tapestry needle, medium
- Sticky tape
- Superglue
- Scissors

Your bracelet will be quite individual; this would be a great way to utilise beads left over from other projects

Blue Bracelet

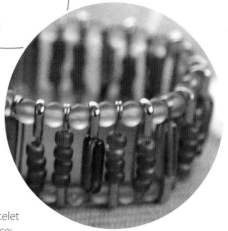

1 Thread the long blue beads onto nine of the safety pins, making sure that they are all securely closed. Assemble the irridescent green beads in groups of four onto the remaining pins then close each pin.

2 Thread the end of the bead elastic through the eye of a tapestry needle. Assemble the bracelet by repeating the following sequence: thread on a turquoise bead, a pin with a blue bead, another turquoise bead, a pin with green beads, another turquoise bead and a second pin with green beads. Position the pins so that all the gems face the same direction and thread them alternately through the loop and the hole in the fastener.

3 When you have threaded on all the pins and beads, as shown, cut the elastic so that there is 5cm (2in) left over at each end and tape the tips together temporarily. Re-thread the needle and pass it through the bottom ends of all the pins, adding a bead between each.

4 Pull up the two ends of the elastic so that the bracelet will fit snugly onto your wrist, but not too tight. Then tie them together with a double reef knot (see page 10). Do the same with the first round of elastic.

5 To finish, dab a small drop of superglue on each knot and allow to dry completely. Then trim the ends of the elastic to 3mm (⅛in) and carefully slide the elastic round so that the knot is concealed.

Green Bracelet

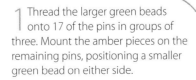

1 Thread the larger green beads onto 17 of the pins in groups of three. Mount the amber pieces on the remaining pins, positioning a smaller green bead on either side.

2 Assemble the bracelet as in step 2 onwards above, threading the two types of pin alternately and adding an irridescent green bead after each one.

Top tip

Look out for the small gold safety pins used for attaching clothes labels to make a delicate version with pearls or metallic beads.

Bead Sparkling

Get set for spring with these designs straight off the catwalk. You've found the perfect outfit, but still need a piece of jewellery to finish it off. Don't resort to paying out for a necklace that you know you will see on three other people in the same day. Instead, try out simple beading techniques and make original, stunning gem sets to match all your favourite threads – in just one evening! With beading being popular at the moment, there is a wide selection to choose from, so you are sure to find something that is 'so you'.

YOU WILL NEED:

- Leather thong, pink, orange, 60cm (24in)
- Beading cord, nylon, 1mm diameter, 20cm (8in)
- Clasps, decorative, silver tone, two; cord, silver, four
- Earring wires, silver, two
- Beads: flower, 10mm (²⁄₅in), four; 7mm (³⁄₁₀in), six
- Headpins: silver, 45mm (2in), nine; 30mm (1⅕in), four
- Beads: orange/gold, 60; glass, round, black, 4mm (³⁄₁₆in), 30; red, round, 4mm (³⁄₁₆in), ten; 8mm (³⁄₈in), eight; pink 4mm (³⁄₁₆in), 12; 8mm (³⁄₈in), six; dark pink 8mm (³⁄₈in), six
- Jump rings, silver, 5mm (⅕in), 17

TOOLS:
- Round-nose pliers
- Wire cutters

Designer
Corinne Bradd

Necklace

The pretty flower beads add a feminine touch to the necklace and earrings, perfect for mum or a special friend

1 Cut a 35cm (13.5in) length of both orange and pink leather thong. Place one set of ends together and insert them into a cord grip. Squeeze with pliers and repeat at the other end. Thread 11 jump rings over the clasp and onto the thong.

2 Place a selection, including one large flower and two large glass beads, onto a 45mm (2in) headpin with a depth of 38mm (1½in). Bend over the end and fix to the centre jump ring. Continue carefully threading pairs onto 45mm (2in) headpins, making each one progressively shorter as you go.

3 Trim the remaining ends of wire to 7mm (³⁄₁₀in), before bending into a loop. Use silver flower beads on the next two, keeping them in line with the first drop. Make a third pair, before switching to

30mm (1⅛in) pins for the last. Fix all three onto the jump rings in order of length.

4 Lay the necklace out flat and pace the drops evenly, to a width of about 10cm (4in). While the jump rings are in position, gently squeeze each one together. Open two more and attach to the cord clasps. Thread a decorative grip onto the rings before closing up.

Top tip

Place a folded towel down before threading the beads to prevent them rolling away.

Bracelet

1 Knot the end of the nylon cord. Cut a 17cm (6½in) length of both orange and pink leather thong. Then place one set of ends together. Insert into a cord clasp and carefully squeeze together with a pair of pliers to close up.

2 Next, thread on a randomly selected mixture of beads, including two small and one large flower. Continue in this way until the string is 15cm (6in) long and then tie the end of the nylon to close.

3 Wrap the two thongs loosely around the string. Trim to the same length as the knot. Clamp all three pieces together with another cord clasp. Open two jump rings slightly and attach to both hooks. To finish, add a decorative fastener and then close up. Your bracelet is now ready to wear.

These pieces would look great with either a floaty dress or smart jeans

Earrings

1 Thread a variety of beads of your choice onto a 45mm (2in) headpin, including one 7mm (³⁄₁₀in) flower, until you reach a length of 30mm (1⅕in). Trim the remaining wire to 7mm (³⁄₁₀in) and bend over with round-nose pliers.

2 Fix a jump ring onto the loop before it is closed up completely. Open slightly and fix an earring wire. Repeat for the second earring.

Top tip

Use a tiny drop of high-tack PVA to ensure the beads don't slide around.

Oriental Charm

Sophisticated beaded and stamped accessories beautifully complete any outfit. These fabulous jewellery items bring elements of the mystical East to any outfit using traditional turquoise and cloisonné beads to accompany crystals and pearls. The earrings are very simple to make, while the brooch is more challenging but perfect for fastening an elegant sarong. Presented on their own Chinese stamped cards why not make a matching greeting card, too?

YOU WILL NEED:

- Wire, gold: 0.6mm (23swg) wide, 3cm (1⅕in); 0.4mm (27swg), 50cm (19.5in)
- Beads, seed, 5g (0.176oz), size 7
- Swarovski crystals, red, eight assorted, 4mm (³⁄₁₆in), 5mm (⅕in), 6mm (¼in)
- Earring wires, four, gold
- Headpins, five, gold
- Tumble chips, seven/eight, large, turquoise
- Beads: cloisonné, three; pearl, round, gold, red, assorted 4mm (³⁄₁₆in), 5mm (⅕in), 30
- Thonging, leather, 0.5m (1ft 6in)
- Cards and envelopes, pre-folded
- Handmade paper, dark red, one sheet
- Polymer clay, red
- Paint, black, acrylic
- Sculpey varnish
- Paper glue
- Assorted Chinese stamps
- Ink pads, black, gold

Tools:
- Wire cutters
- Round-nose pliers

Designer
Jema Hewitt

Cards

1 Cut a rectangle of the handmade paper, 4.4cm (1⅖in) x 7cm (2¾in), and glue to the front of a card, positioning it towards the top left-hand corner. Leave a 1cm (½in) gap around the top and left edges.

2 On the bottom right corner of the card, use the Chinese stamps to create a vintage luggage label effect, overlapping and layering different ones in both black and gold inks. Allow them to creep over onto the handmade paper, but not too far. To attach a piece of jewellery, make a small hole in the front of the card with a bradawl and thread the wires or cord through.

Pendant

1 Roll out a small piece of sculpey to 0.5cm (⅕in) thick. Cover with cling film and use the blunt side of a 2cm (¾in) circle cutter to create a shape. It should not cut the film, but create a lovely domed design. Peel off the film and lightly make your motif using the stamps – use a texture stamp followed by a slightly deeper imprint of a symbol for maximum effect. Make a very small hole at the top of the pendant and carefully bake according to the manufacturers' instructions.

2 When cool, brush on a thick coating of runny black acrylic paint. Immediately wipe most of it off, leaving some paint to create darker shading in the imprinted areas. When dry, give it a good layer of varnish.

3 To make the necklace, thread an oval jump ring through the pendant and close by twisting. On an eyepin, thread a size 7 seed bead either side of a turquoise chip and create a top loop, as for the earrings. Thread the pendant's jump ring on one end and a length of leather thong onto the other. Knot and secure to finish.

Top tip

Two-piece sieve findings are available for earrings and necklace clasps too – create a whole matching set of jewellery using the same techniques.

Even if you're not planning an exotic holiday you're sure to feel the lure of the Orient

Earrings

1 For the first pair of earrings, thread a 4mm (³⁄₁₆in) red bead, a 4mm (³⁄₁₆in) gold one, long cloisonné gem, then a gold and a red bead onto each of the two head pins. For the second pair, thread a red 4mm (³⁄₁₆in), a turquoise chip, a round gold 4mm (³⁄₁₆in), a 5mm (¹⁄₅in) crystal, another round gold 4mm (³⁄₁₆in), then finish with three size 7 turquoise seed beads.

2 To create the top loop, grip the round-nose pliers about 3mm (¹⁄₁₀in) from the top bead. Twist the pliers through 90 degrees away from you, creating a right angle. With your free hand, curve the top piece of the headpin back towards you, shaping it tightly over the top of the pliers.

3 Keep curving until it crosses the other piece of wire then remove the round-nose pliers.

Slide the wire cutters inside the loop so the cutting edge is flush with the inside edge of the wire circle, and snip. Open the earring wires loop by twisting, and thread on the headpin. Twist once more to close.

Brooch

1 Onto the 0.6mm (23swg) wire, thread two turquoise size 7 seeds, two round gold beads and two more size 7 seeds. Curve the wire slightly and pass each end down through a hole at the edge of the sieve piece. Bend the wire at a right angle at the back of the sieve to secure, creating a loop from which you hang the dangling piece.

2 Take the 0.4mm (27swg) wire and thread it up through one of the edge holes from the back of the sieve finding, leaving a 3cm (1⅛in) tail. Thread on a tumble chip and pass back down through another hole. Bring up through a different one and then continue adding beads all around the sieve in the same way as before.

3 You can thread on more than one gem at once, but make sure the sieve is completely and densely covered. To finish off, pass the wire down to the back and twist it together with the 3cm (1⅛in) tail you originally left. Trim the wires and attach the back of the sieve fastening carefully, to finish.

Top tip

Small cutters can be purchased from sugar craft suppliers whose assorted tools are ideal for working with polymer clays such as sculpey.

Cool Jewels

Every woman needs a bit of bling in their lives to make them feel truly special. Get your fix with this fabulous beaded jewellery and brooch set. Diamonds may be a girl's best friend but you'll have much more fun with these little gems. Holographic plastic and divine beads allow you to be truly individual, making your jewellery as glamorous or as low key as you desire. And making it couldn't be simpler. The hardest part is choosing out of all the available colours and designs!

YOU WILL NEED:
• Beads, seed, assorted glass, large flat plastic
• Holographic plastic sheet, pink, red, clear
• Chiffon ribbon, scraps
• Net, pink
• Monofilament thread, fine
• Needle, fine
• Elastic thread, clear, 0.8mm (21swg)
• Brooch bars, small
• Nail varnish, clear

Tools:
• Plier punch
• Scissors, small

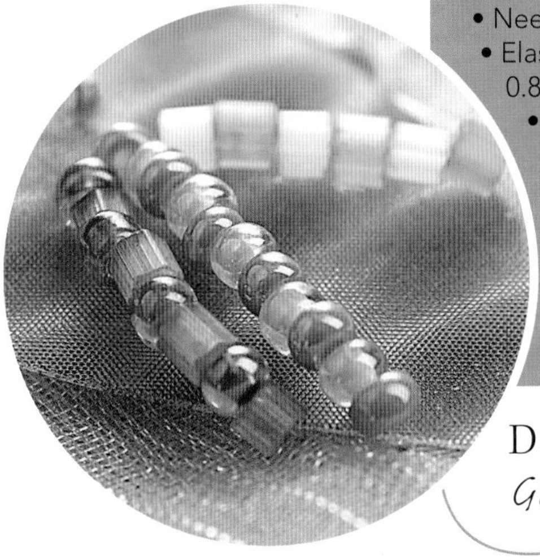

Designer
Glennis Gilruth

Flower Brooch and Bracelet

1 Cut an oval of clear plastic and punch holes all over. Using monofilament and a needle, sew a pink pearl in the centre then add yellow droplet beads around it to form flower petals.

2 Cover the remaining background with pink and lilac satin seed beads. Add a few pink seeds randomly around the central pearl. Sew a small brooch bar on the reverse.

3 Make a matching bracelet using the same beads and stretch elastic. Thread seed beads as usual but tie the thread after each pearl or droplet (see diagram, page 119).

Heart Brooch and Bracelet

1 Tear a scrap of netting. Trim three scraps of pale green chiffon ribbon and fray the edges. Layer together, stitching in the middle to secure. Cut a heart shape from the holographic plastic (see diagram, page 119).

2 Place the plastic heart in the centre of the fabric, securing with three strands of seed beads threaded onto fine monofilament. Decorate with extra bead and fasten.

3 Create a matching bracelet by threading together seed beads and assorted glass beads alternately through stretch elastic. After each group of seed beads or glass bead, tie a secure knot (see diagram, page 119). Tie a few scraps of pink net between the beads.

Top tip

To ensure that your knots are secure, be sure to follow the instructions on the elastic bead cord packaging

Pink Stripe and Bracelet

1 Cut a wavy edged square from pink holographic plastic (see diagram, page 119) and make holes along the edge with a plier punch. Using fine monofilament and a needle, make strings of seed beads between the holes, and then add flat, round beads between each string. Try to restrict the stitches on the reverse of the brooch to the edges. Glue a small brooch bar on the back.

2 Make a matching bracelet by threading seed beads and flat round beads onto stretch elastic. Make the flat beads stand out by tying a knot after each one (see diagram, page 119).

Card

1 Trim a flower shape from plastic using small curved scissors and make a hole in the centre with a darning needle. Create a stem from green paper yarn or similar, tie a knot and thread the flower and a sequin onto it. Neatly trim the yarn close to the knot.

2 Make up a beaded flowerpot in a similar fashion to the pink stripe brooch. Assemble the motif on the front of the card using sticky foam pads, and add leaves cut from plastic.

3 Cut notches in the top and bottom of the card, close to the fold. String assorted beads onto clear cord, knotting in between each group, and position on the card using the notches to hold it in place. Tie the cord on the inside to secure them.

Bracelet

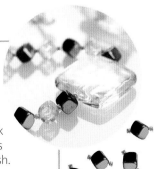

1 Work stretch elastic through a flat, square bead. Add black and clear cube beads, placing pink seed beads between, knot threads together and then dab with varnish.

2 Complete the look by threading up a matching brooch, gluing a small brooch bar on the reverse.

Top tip

For a professional finish, ensure all yarn is neatly trimmed close to knots.

Helter-Skelter

This gorgeous design makes the most of silver wire spiralling around pretty gems. You can experiment with different types and colours of gemstones to go in the middle for an extra-special effect. Finish off with a delicate spiral at the bottom to sparkle against your hair. The ideal accessory for a party, night out on the town or any special occasion, this perfectly matched pair will look great with any outfit and is sure to guarantee you compliments all night!

Designer
Linda Jones

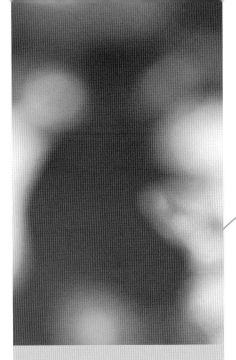

YOU WILL NEED:

- Seed beads, one larger bead (about 8–10cm (3–4in), 0.8mm (¹⁄₁₆in) (21swg)
- Silver wire
- Two earring wires

Tools:

- Round- and flat-nose pliers
- Wire cutters

Earrings

1 Working directly from a spool of 0.8mm (21swg) wire, form a small circle at the end, using the tips of your round-nose pliers. Hold this circle firmly in your flat-nose pliers, and then continue curling the wire around itself to form a tight spiral, which is approximately 10cm (4in) in diameter.

2 Snip the wire from the spool, using your cutters, leaving 10cm (4in) projecting from the spiral. Place the tip of your round-nose pliers in the centre of the spiral and stretch the coils out, creating an even space between them. Use your fingers and finger nails to separate each coil, until the tapered spiral is approximately 20cm (8in) long.

3 Pull and straighten some 0.8mm (21swg) wire from your spool and thread it into the centre of your tapered, spiral coil, starting at the widest end. Create a link at the end of the narrowest part of the spiral coil, using the tips of your round-nose pliers.

4 Cut the wire off the spool leaving approximately 15cm (6in) projecting past the top of the widest part of the coil. Then thread the centre wire with beads, starting with small seed beads and ending with the larger bead.

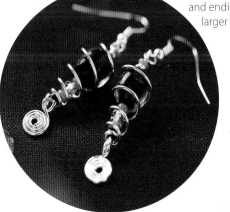

5 Wrap the end of the spiral coil wire around the central wire to secure, just by the bead hole. Thread a small bead onto the top projecting wire and create a link, using the tips of your round-nose pliers.

6 Create another small, tight spiral (following steps 1–3) with 0.8mm (21swg) wire. Then create a link at the end with the tips of your round-nose pliers. Connect this to the link at the narrow end of your tapered, spiral coil and an ear wire at the opposite end. Repeat all the above steps to create a pair of earrings!

Top tip

Make bigger spirals for larger gems and beads by wrapping wire around other objects such as a pencil.

Iced Gems

Busy Beads

Add some glamour to your summer wardrobe with glitzy gems. All girls like to wear a bit of jewellery now and again, but most of us struggle to find the money for decent looking accessories on a budget, so if you enjoy beading, why not have a go at these sparklers. It's a fun pastime you can do anywhere, even in the garden on a sunny day, and the perfect way to match colour schemes to suit particular outfits.

YOU WILL NEED:
- Wire, silver-plated, 0.6mm (23swg)
- Crimps, silver
- Earring wires, silver
- Beads: seed; cylinder, 15mm (⅗in); rice, 6mm (¼in); flat, oval; chip beads, 9mm (⅖in); crystal, 7mm (³⁄₁₀in)
- Silicone thread
- Spring clasp

Tools:
- Pliers: round-nose; flat-nose
- Wire cutters

Designer
Dorothy Wood

Basic Necklace and Bracelet Links

1 To make a basic link for necklaces and bracelets, cut 15cm (6in) of 0.6mm (23swg) silver-plated wire. Place in the jaws of round-nose pliers, 5mm (⅕in) from the tips and bend around the blades, using your thumb, then remove. A ring should have been formed at the end.

2 Hold the ring with the pliers and bend the tail back slightly to straighten. Pick up selected beads. To make the ring at the other end, place in the pliers 5mm (⅕in) from the tips again and bend the wire around, then pull the tail down straight and snip.

3 Grasp the ring in flat-nose pliers and bend back to straighten. Hold both ends of the link between finger and thumb, and twist until they are level. Make enough to go around your wrist or neck and join together. To open the links, hold at one end in flat-nose pliers and bend up. Bend down to close.

Green Necklace

Make 18 basic links using 0.6mm (23swg) silver-plated wire, and thread a pale green crystal, a dark green rice bead and another crystal. Then, make five with a long cylinder. Join seven crystal links together and add a cylinder bead piece followed by a crystal one. Repeat until all five are interspaced with crystal links.

Finish with the remaining basic ones. Attach a spring clasp to one end and a jump ring to the other. To do so, hold the links at one end in flat-nose pliers and bend up, then bend down to close.

Depending on time, you can make individual items or a whole co-ordinating set

Top tip

When joining links, do not pull the ring open sideways as this distorts the round shape.

Blue and Green Necklace

1 Make six basic links with three seed beads, a blue flat oval, a blue 5mm (⅕in) crystal, another oval and three more seeds. Thread five more sets with pale green. Join in alternating colours. Create three pieces with three seed beads, a blue crystal and three more seeds, and another three with pale blue in the same formation.

2 Join three basic links to either end of the necklace. To make some dangly links, use seed beads and add weight by threading on 7mm (¹⁄₁₀in) crystals and 9mm (⅖in) chip beads. Create nine in graduated sizes and attach, as shown.

Earrings

For dangly earrings, make up a basic link for the top half. For the lower piece add larger gems, such as cylinders or chip beads then a crimp at the other end. Do this by squeezing closed with flat-nose pliers, then snip off any excess.

Bracelet

1 The bracelet is made using silicone thread, which is thick enough to use without a needle. Unwind the tail, pick up three or four seed beads, then a large decorative one. Repeat until it is the length that you want to go around your wrist.

2 Tie the ends together with 11 or 12 reef knots (see page 10), then trim. Make an assortment of lower links as for the earrings, then open the wire ring and loop it over the bracelet between beads and close. Your bracelet is now complete and ready to wear.

Top tip

For a nicely balanced earring, make the top link with small and medium beads then add one or two larger gems to add weight to the bottom part.

79

Iced Sparkle

There is an enticing selection of beautiful gems widely available today. This lovely set incorporates lots of different styles, so it is a great way of using examples you have just a couple of, or recycling old broken accessories. It is also a very good excuse for buying a few new beads that catch your eye. Create a unique necklace using an array of eyecatching beads, or if you are short for time, it is easy to make a beautiful bracelet, earrings or even a matching handbag charm. Or why not indulge yourself by creating a unique co-ordinating set, to use up all those leftover beads?

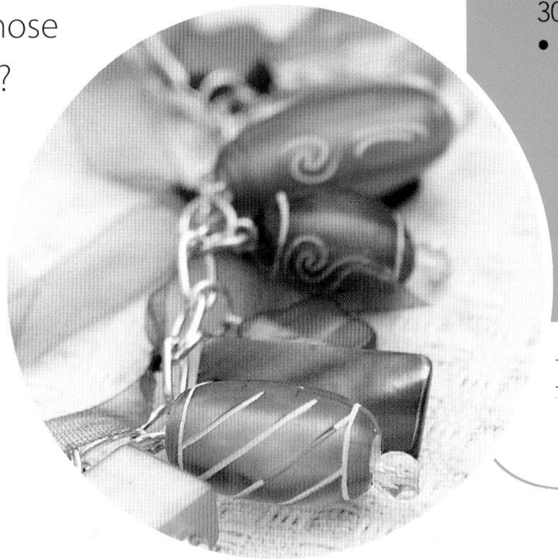

YOU WILL NEED:

YOU WILL NEED:

- Cable chain, 60cm (24in)
- Headpins, silver, 40
- Jump rings, silver, 4mm (³⁄₁₆in), 8mm (³⁄₈in)
- Toggle necklace clasps
- Assortments of beads: cubes, pink 1cm (½in); glass diamond, blue 1.5cm (⅝in); mother-of-pearl, pink 1.1cm (½in); glass tube 2cm (¾in); plastic lozenges, blue 2.5cm (1in), grey, 1.5cm (⅝in), lilac,1.8cm (1¹⁄₁₆in); rocaille, pink, 6mm (¼in)
- Organza ribbon, lilac
- Earring wires, kidney silver, 30cm (11²⁄₅in)
- Key ring

Tools:
- Wire cutters
- Round-nose pliers

Designer
Cheryl Owen

Necklace

1 Each bead needs to be hung on a headpin. If the holes are too large, thread a smaller one on first, i.e. a pale pink rocaille followed by a pink cube, or a 4mm (³⁄₁₆in) round clear plastic bead, then a blue glass diamond or lozenge (see the photo for reference).

2 Snip the wire of the headpin 1cm (½in) above the bead. Bend the extending piece into a loop with a pair of round-nose pliers. Slip the loop of each headpin onto a jump ring. Hang the tags on jump rings. Cut the ribbon into five, 10cm (4in) lengths. Tie each one round a jump ring with a tight knot at the centre. Cut the extending the ends diagonally, 3cm (1⅛in) long.

3 Arrange the beads, tags and ribbons in a row in a pleasing mix of shapes and colours. Snip a 44cm (17½in) length of chain with wire cutters. Working outwards from the centre, fix each jump ring onto a chain link and close securely. Attach a jump ring to each end of the chain then add on a toggle necklace clasp.

Bracelet

1 To make the matching bracelet, fix each bead onto a headpin, then hang on a jump ring, following the steps as before with the necklace. Arrange the beads, discs and dragonflies in a row, until you are satisfied with the appearance of the bracelet.

2 Then, working outwards from the centre of a 16cm (6³⁄₁₀in) chain, fix each jump ring onto a chain link and close securely. To finish, attach a jump ring to each end of the chain then carefully fasten on a toggle necklace clasp.

Top tip

If you do not have wire cutters, use an old pair of scissors to snip wire, but not a new pair as this will blunt the blades.

Earrings

1 A gorgeous pair of matching earrings would go really well with the necklace and bracelet set. For each earring, simply slip one flower, one glass gem onto a headpin. Follow this by adding four rocaille beads on as well.

2 Then carefully snip the wire 1cm (½in) above the last bead. Bend the extending wire into a loop with a pair of round-nose pliers, to finish, then slip onto an earring wire. Feel free to experiment with any designs that you wish, simply by varying the types or colours of beads used in the design.

Handbag Charm

Why not make a matching handbag charm? You'll need some silver thread and a little clear nail varnish in addition to the beads.

1 Dab a little clear nail varnish onto the ends of a length of silver thread to stiffen and make it easier to pass through the beads. Leave to dry. Tie the centre of the thread securely to an 8mm (⅜in) jump ring.

2 Fit ten round clear plastic beads onto one thread and 12 on the other. Add a glass frosted white bead, then a pale pink pearl and a butterfly onto each. Tie securely under each motif and cut off the excess.

Top tip

Open a jump ring sideways, don't open outwards as it may snap. Secure jump rings closed with a little superglue or clear nail varnish.

Charm School

Combine shiny glass beads and charms with coloured cord for super-trendy jewellery. Don't spend a fortune on designer jewels when you can make your own to look just as good. Bright glass beads, hooked onto a silver chain and finished with a fancy finding, become a jangly fashion statement, while shells and charms grouped and strung on cord give a sophisticated look. Complete the effect with a swinging necklace that's a combination of cord and chain with loads of beautiful beads.

YOU WILL NEED:

- Beads: art glass; glass, shell discs, seed
- Charms
- Headpins
- Jump rings
- Clasps: lobster; chain; toggle
- Crimps, leather
- Pliers
- Wire cutters
- Epoxy resin

Designer
Allison Galpin

Art Glass Bracelet

1 Cut a chain to your bracelet size. Add two jump rings at either end and attach the bar of a toggle clasp to one side, and a loop to the other. Thread a seed bead onto a headpin. Add the main art glass bead charm, then another seed bead. Cut the headpin with pliers, leaving 1cm (½in) exposed.

2 Grip the wire at the base of the exposed headpin and bend at a right angle using round-nose pliers. Form a loop by twisting your wrist in the opposite direction. Thread this hook onto the fourth chain link, and close the loop securely with pliers. Repeat the process every three to four links of your chain, to create the pattern, as shown in the photograph.

Shell Charm Bracelet

1 Cut two co-ordinating shades of 3mm (¹⁄₁₀in) flat suede cord to your bracelet length. Knot them together every 4cm (1½in). Place each end into leather crimps and squeeze them together with pliers until the suede is gripped tightly.

2 Attach a jump ring at either side of the crimps and add a lobster clasp to one end. Decorate the knots with co-ordinating shell discs and leaf bead charms. Finally attach metal charms via jump rings, to the spaces between the knots.

Top tip

With round-nose pliers, the thinner the tip the better.

Vine necklace

1 Knot two pieces of 3mm-
(⅛in) wide suede at either
end of a necklace connector.
Attach clasps as before. Cut
an 8cm (3in) fine link chain
and decorate with 6mm (¼in)
cat's eye beads, leaf beads,
silver pebble charm drops and
assorted mixed glass versions in
co-ordinating colours.

2 Place the beads in an
irregular fashion in groups
of three, two and an occasional
single charm, in different links.
End the chain with a pebble
drop. Attach the other end of the
chain, through a jump ring, to
the centre of the connector, and
put shell discs either side. Finish
with two coin charms.

*Experiment with
various different beads
and colours for
exciting looks. Try
using red glass beads
for a festive feel*

Top tip

*For super-secure fastenings,
use a drop of epoxy resin
on your leather crimps to fix
them tightly.*

Good Times

You'll never be late for an important date with this watch strap you'll be proud to show off. Complement that little black dress with stunning jewels that are as practical as they are eye-catching. If you can't run to buying real sapphires and diamonds for a celebration, we've got the most desirable alternative around. Once you start creating your own designer jewellery you'll be amazed by the flattering remarks you'll receive everywhere you go, and you'll soon be making personalized gifts that all your friends and family will treasure for years to come.

Designer
Corinne Bradd

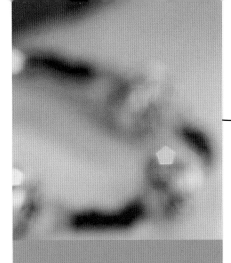

Watch

1 Working on a flat surface, begin by opening two jump rings by 1mm (1/16in) and attaching to each lug on the watch face. Thread three eyepins (those with loops at the end) onto each ring and close up.

2 Add an assortment of smaller beads, 20mm (3/4in) long, onto each pin, working on one side at a time, then bend the remaining 7mm (2 3/4in) to make a loop. Before closing each one, thread another eyepin for the next section.

3 Continue with each chain until they reach 60–70mm (2 1/2–2 3/4in), varying the size of the beads and making some sections shorter by cutting 5–10mm (1/5– 2/5in) off the end of the eyepin before threading. Finish each side of the strap with loops and then attach them to a jump ring.

4 Fasten the clasp to one end of the strap and the chain to the other, then check the fit of the watch before you carry on. Adjustments can be made by unbending joins and taking off beads. Trim the eyepin by a few millimetres before reforming the loop.

5 Thread assorted beads onto headpins, trim and bend the end to form a loop. Fix to an existing hoop on the strap before closing up fully. Make these attachments the desired length by cutting the headpin down to 20mm (3/4in) and threading on a few beads. Bend the loop and join a shortened eyepin, then thread a few gems onto this and fasten to the strap as before.

YOU WILL NEED:

- Quartz watch, decorative, modern 22mm (3/4in)
- Beads: faceted, glass, 6mm (1/4in), aqua; round, silver, 12mm; oval line pattern, silver, 22mm (3/4in); glass, blue, handmade assortment
- Pins: eye, silver, 30mm (1 1/5in); head, silver, 30mm (1 1/5in)
- Jump rings, silver, 6mm (1/4in) diameter
- Chain and clasp, silver
- Beading elastic, clear, 1mm

Tools:

- Pliers, round-nose
- Wire cutters

Once you have the hang of this beading technique you will be amazed what else you can create

Bracelets

1 Cut a 22cm (8 7/10in) length of medium thickness clear beading elastic and tie a loose knot at one end. Thread a large oval handmade glass bead and three smaller faceted gems onto this, repeating until the bracelet measures 18cm (7in).

2 Stretch the elastic and double knot the ends, ensuring the initial knot is outside of this. Trim close to the knot and, if possible, manipulate the beads so that it is covered by a large glass oval one.

Silver Bracelet

Make as before, but thread a large round decorative silver gem flanked by a smaller faceted one and five seed beads.

Top tip

Long, thin tweezers are very useful for holding jump rings and eyepins securely while attaching other elements.

Simply Charming

Get set for the sun with our beautiful trinkets. We all have things that we love best about each season. In winter it may be snug boots, scarves, puddings or generally feeling cosy. Now in the summer there is so much to look forward to; the heat on your face, bare feet and wearing colourful clothes to name just a few. Whether you're off on holiday to enjoy warmer climates or simply want to adorn your arms, a bracelet can liven up any outfit. Beads are as popular as ever and these pretty bracelets will look great teamed with a sarong or floaty dress. If you want to create a batch from different colours, or give some to your friends, there is also the choice of a simpler version. So go on, get yourself in the mood, it is sure to make you feel brighter!

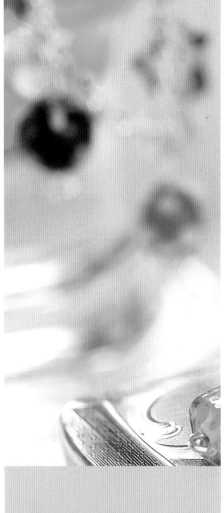

YOU WILL NEED:

- Wire, silver, 0.8mm, (21swg)
- Beads: glass, assorted, turquoise; seed, turquoise, white

Tools:
- Pliers: round-nose; flat-nose
- Wire cutters
- Dowel, cylindrical or thick knitting needle

Designer
Linda Jones

Bracelet

Pretty beads are the perfect way to add a little colour to an outfit and can instantly update your look

1 Thread a large turquoise bead with 0.8mm (21swg) silver wire. Place onto the end and form a little hook with round-nose pliers, squeeze this back onto itself with flat-nose pliers. Curl tightly around to make a small spiral. Repeat several times.

2 Push the bead up to the spiral, leaving 1.5cm (⅝in) extending from the hole, and cut the wire off the spool. Using the tips of round-nose pliers, bend this extended piece 90º, squeezing the end tightly. Curl it back towards the top of the bead, moulding it around the shaft of the pliers to form a top link.

3 Thread 15–20 of the smaller seed beads individually onto 0.8mm (21swg) wire, forming loops at the ends of each. Make others into groups of three, with

spirals as the end terminals. Wrap more wire around a cylindrical dowel or thick knitting needle to make nine circles. Remove this 'spring' then snip each off.

4 Thread the wire circles with the units made before, forming bunches of suspended beads. Attach the rings to each other with threaded seed beads to create a chain. The amount of sections needed depends on the length of the overall bracelet required.

5 Create a fish hook clasp by curling 0.8mm (21swg) wire into a small circle with round-nose pliers. Next, place the pliers just under this and bend in the opposite direction on the widest part of the tool. Cut off the spool, leaving 1.5cm (⅝in), and carefully create a link at the end to finish. Alternatively, use ready-made fittings.

Top tip

Wire spirals are a very effective card decoration! Create them in any colour, size, or gauge for alternative looks to your cards.

Easy Peasy ⟩ Card

For a simpler design, use an 18cm (7in) length of ready-made chain and add a clasp at each end. Suspend this with threaded 'bobbly' beads, leaving even spaces in between. In the gaps, link wire spirals, as described previously, for added decoration.

1 Create spiral shapes as before, varying the 'open' and 'closed' design. These are made in the same way, except the latter has a space between each layer. When you have made them to your preferred size, bend the ends 90°.

2 Cut out a rectangle of navy card with deckle-edged scissors. Push each coil into this panel, squeezing it flat to secure, then cover the back with masking tape so that it cannot swivel or fall out. Mount with 3-D pads on a yellow blank.

This unusual spiral technique can be used on anything from beaded jewellery to greetings cards

Top tip

To strengthen your spirals and to stop them from bending, work on a steel block.

Glitter Ball

Crafting individually designed pieces not only creates a sense of achievement but also fabulous additions to any wardrobe! This stunning pendant perfectly complements any outfit – just choose your favourite coloured gems and attach to the chain of your choice. The focal point of your look, this necklace will make sure you turn heads wherever you go!

YOU WILL NEED:
- 0.8mm (21swg) silver wire
- 0.6mm (23swg) silver wire
- Seed beads
- One focal bead

Tools:
- Round- and flat-nose pliers
- Wire cutters

Designer
Linda Jones

1 Thread your focal bead with 0.8mm (23swg) wire, forming two small links using your round-nose pliers, at each end of the bead. Make sure the links are all facing in the same direction.

2 Thread 0.6mm (21swg) wire through one of the links and bring the wire around the circumference of the bead to encircle it. Cut the wire off the spool, allowing enough to encircle, plus an extra 30cm (12in). Thread this wire with small seed beads on each side of the link, until the bead is fully framed.

3 Thread one of the wires through one side of the top link and the other through the opposite side, and twist where they meet to secure. Wrap one wire around the other stem and cut off any excess, leaving only one projecting wire. Then, using your fingers, spend a little time moulding the bead frame around the focal bead.

4 Use the end of your round-nose pliers (or a cylindrical mandrel such as knitting needle), to curl a 5cm (2in) tight, even coil of 0.8mm (21swg) wire. Then thread this coil onto the top of the projecting 0.6mm (23swg) wire. This will act as a sleeve, covering the wrapped wires underneath.

5 Thread one more bead on top of the coil and form a wrapped loop with the projecting 0.6mm (23swg) wire. Create this by placing your round-nose pliers just by the top bead and wrapping the wire around the circular shaft, wrapping it where it forms a complete link to secure.

6 Connect the pendant onto a chain, ribbon or cord of your choice to finish.

Top tip

Gently tap the end of the top loop with a hammer on a steel block to harden the ends of the circular shaft.

Pearly Power

Pearly Queen

Whatever the occasion, these delicate accessories are sure to be a hit! Pearls have been used to make bridal jewellery for many years, and are a simple way to add an elegant touch to the wedding dress. There's no need to break the budget either, as imitation gems look just like the real thing. With the use of simple filigree caps you can create a wonderful antique feel and, rather than stringing the beads on thread, use silver-plated wire and chain for a contemporary effect.

YOU WILL NEED:

- Wire, silver-plated, 0.6mm (23swg)
- Chain, silver-plated: light-weight; medium-weight
- Pearls, 8mm (⅜in), 10mm (⅖in), ivory, pale blue, pale green
- Beads: cubes, 6mm (¼in), pale blue, pale green; silver-plated, grooved, round, oval; crystal, faceted, 8mm (⅜in), 10mm (⅖in), pale blue; seed beads
- Filigree caps, silver-plated, 7mm (¾₀in), 10mm (⅖in)
- Headpins, silver-plated
- Clasp: necklace, heart-shaped; jewellery
- Jump rings
- Earring wires, sterling silver

Tools:
- Pliers: round-nose; flat-nose
- Wire cutters

Designer
Dorothy Wood

A charm bracelet is very personal and can be used to remember various stages of your life

Top tip

Don't pull the loop open or you will distort the shape; simply hold in the pliers and push up or down, reversing to close.

Necklace

1 To make the basic link for the necklace, bracelet and earrings, cut a 25cm (10in) length of 0.6mm (23swg) silver-plated wire. Hold in the round-nose pliers, 5mm (⅛in) from the tips so that you can just feel the end of the wire. Carefully twist the length around the jaws until it touches its end, making a lop-sided ring.

2 Put the pliers in the loop again and bend the tail back slightly to straighten. You should now have a ring on the end of the wire. Pick up three different beads; if you use a pearl at the end, put a filigree cap over the tip before threading onto the wire.

3 To make the loop at the other end, hold in the round-nose pliers, 5mm (⅛in) from the end with the tail sticking upwards and the jaws just 1mm (¹⁄₁₆in)

from the last bead. Wind around to make a loop. Trim off the end as close as you can, using the tips of the wire cutters.

4 For the necklace, you will need nine, three-bead links. Make some ivory, some blue and others pale green, adding metal gems for variety. Create 13 wire links in the same way, with only one bead in them.

5 Arrange the larger links in two rows – three in the top and four along the bottom. Position a single bead link between each larger one, and with another at each end. Using flat-nose pliers, open the loop at one end of each, fix on the next link and close up.

6 Cut two pieces of chain with three links and two with eight links. Attach the short lengths to each end of the longer necklace

and vice versa. Next, fix both chains at one end to a single bead link and repeat at the other end (these could both be oval metal gems).

7 Trim four pieces of chain with four links and two lengths, 6.5cm (³⁄₁₀in) each. Attach a short section to either end of the necklace, then a three bead link, followed by another short piece. Finally attach a single bead link and the longer lengths of chain. Finish with a gorgeous heart-shaped fastening, attached using jump rings.

Charm Bracelet

1 Using the basic technique explained in steps one and two on page 100, make five single bead links with large 10mm (²⁄₅in) pearls and faceted crystals. Add filigree caps to one end of each. Cut four, seven-link lengths of medium-weight chain. Open the rings at the end of the bead links and attach chain between each one to create the bracelet.

2 For the charms, pick up an 8mm (³⁄₈in) or 10mm (²⁄₅in) bead on the end of a headpin. Hold the pin's tail in round-nose pliers so that the wire is 5mm (¹⁄₅in) from the end and there is a 1mm (¹⁄₁₆in) gap between the jaws and the gem. Bend the tail around the pliers to make a loop. Trim end with cutters, then straighten by pulling back a little.

3 Make 16 single gem charms using a variety of different

gems. If the headpin pulls through the hole, thread on a tiny seed bead first. Attach four charms to the middle of each chain, on adjacent links to form a cluster. Check the length on your wrist then fix a short chain to each end and a bracelet fastening using jump rings.

Earrings

1 Using the basic techniques explained above, make two single links with 6mm (¹⁄₄in) ivory pearls. Pick up a 10mm (²⁄₅in) faceted crystal on a headpin, then an oval ribbed metal bead and an 8mm (³⁄₈in) ivory pearl. Using round-nose pliers, bend the wire into a loop and trim off the tail.

2 Straighten the loop with flat-nose pliers. Make a second headpin link in the same way and attach the single pearl links. Fix an earring wire to each of the pearl links to finish.

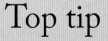

Top tip

Use different coloured beads to create a stunning set to match a favourite outfit.

Glam Rock

With the festive party scene in full swing, a choice of jewellery for dressing up that little black number is essential. Although there are a wealth of cheap and cheerful trinkets on the high street, you can't beat the sense of satisfaction achieved when you've designed your very own bespoke adornments. The simple knotting techniques give the design an original and slightly Oriental flair, which works equally well with jeans or sophisticated evening wear.

YOU WILL NEED:
- Cord, satin, lilac
- Jump rings
- Chain, silver, coloured
- Beads: glass, silver lined pink, lime green calotte, large, silver
- Headpins, silver
- Clasp, lobster
- Eye ring hooks
- Spotty fabric
- Ribbon
- Matching thread

Tools:
- Pliers, small-pointed
- Scissors
- Safety pin
- Sewing machine

Designer
Amanda Walker

Necklace

1 Thread a silver-lined glass bead onto a headpin. Add a lime green bead and then another silver-lined one. Take the pliers and cut off the top of the head pin leaving 1cm (⅖in) extending from the last bauble.

2 Using the point of the pliers, bend the pin over to form an eye. Repeat, threading a pink bead between the two silver-lined sparklers to make another pin with a pink centre.

3 Using the pliers, open a jump ring and thread on the three beaded headpins you have just prepared. Secure by closing the jump ring. Make up another six clusters in the same manner, then two further arrangements with just silver-lined and pink beads. Shape one large cluster containing two pins with silver-lined and green beads, and four using silver and pink.

4 Cut a length of lilac satin cord and find the centre. Make a knot either side of this middle point. Tie eight more knots at four intervals of 2cm (¾in) on each side. Open out the jump ring of the large cluster of beads. Close it over the cord between the two centre knots.

5 Apply six of the green and pink smaller clusters above six of the knots. Attach three either side of the centre knots and the pink clusters to the two remaining knots. Cut a 10cm (4in) length of silver chain. Fix the jump ring to each end. Attach two clusters either side of the centre, then fix the remaining beads to the chain. Cut off any excess length from the two ends of the cord. Tie knots at the tips and encase them with calottes using the pliers. Finally apply a jump to each of the end beads, and a lobster clasp to one of them.

Bracelet

1 Follow the necklace instructions for making up the clusters of beads, forming one large cluster and two smaller green and pink clusters. Cut a length of cord and tie two knots either side of the centre point.

2 Apply the large cluster between them. Make two more knots 2cm (¾in) from either side of the centre and attach the two smaller clusters above them. Tie two more knots, 2cm (¾in) away from the previous ones, and cut off the excess cord. Using the pliers, encase the knots with calottes.

3 Fix a jump ring to one end of two short lengths of silver chain. Attach a lobster clasp to one of the rings and fasten the hook to the second one. Check the finished length. Measure the knotted cord and, if needed,

Top tip

Measure the width of your wrist first to ensure the finished length of the bracelet is suitable for you.

adjust the chain. Attach the jump ring to the chain ends and connect rings to the two calottes.

to each of the beads. See the techniques section on page 17 for further guidance.

Earrings

1 Make up two smaller clusters, following the instructions for the necklace on page 104, threading a lime green bead and pink beads between the two silver lined sparklers as in steps one and two. Next, cut two short lengths of cord and tie a knot both sides of the centre point. Then arrange the clusters in between the knots.

2 Carefully draw the two ends of the cord together and encase inside a calotte. To finish the earrings, attach a silver coloured jump ring and a silver coloured earring hook

Spotty Bag

If you're giving these twisty silk show-stoppers away as a gift, make a matching bag to present them in.

1 Cut a rectangle of spotty fabric 18 x 26cm (7¹⁄₁₀ x 10¹⁄₅in). Fold in half and stitch down the side and across the base to form a bag. Fold in 0.5cm (¹⁄₅in) and then a further 3cm (1¹⁄₅in) around the top of the bag. Edge stitch the 0.5cm (¹⁄₅in) fold forming a hem. Make another row of stitching 1cm (²⁄₅in) above the first forming a channel. Turn the bag to the right side and press.

2 Unpick a few stitches in between the channel on the side seam. Using a safety pin attached to a length of ribbon, thread the tip into the gap and around the top of the bag. Tie the ends together to make the drawstring.

Top tip

To completely change the feel of this design use black cord and pearls for a dramatic evening look.

Flower Power

Make a head-turning necklace that will have friends gasping in amazement. This beautiful accessory is perfect for summer, with its fresh and vibrant aquamarine hues. While it may be wonderfully ornate, it's actually a lot easier to create than it looks. As the beads are simply strung on wire, it requires little in the way of jewellery making tools, and comes in a handy kit too. We're sure crafters of all abilities will enjoy constructing this modern floral design.

Top tip

Keep the wire pulled taut when stringing on beads to make it easier.

Designer
Margo Van Engelen at Avec

Necklace

1 To make the flower motif, cut 20cm (8in) of metal wire and string on 12 wooden rocailles. Form a circle, thread the end through the beads once again and pull taut. Trim 50cm (19½in) of wire and pass through a shell. Insert into one of the gems then come back out.

2 Thread again, going from the back to the front through another shell, skipping one rocaille in the ring. Continue so you have six shells, each overlapping slightly. Pass once again through all gems, for extra firmness. To fasten, insert the ends into several beads in the chain then trim the excess. Repeat for the smaller circle.

3 To make the shorter, less ornate necklace, cut 75cm (29½in) of lime, coated metal wire. String on a silver foil bead and slide it to the middle. Thread 13 rocailles, and insert through the large gem again. Make sure both ends are even. Add nine more, and pass into the centrepiece. Pull taut, creating a circle shape.

4 Finish one half as follows: string on three rocailles and the following glass beads, always with a rocaille in between; large green pearl, medium-sized glass, large light green glass, small green pearl, small glass, large aqua pearl, small glass, medium-sized glass, small green pearl, large dark green glass, small aqua pearl, small glass, medium-sized glass, and small glass bead. Finish the other side in the same way.

5 To make the flower necklace, cut two 75cm (29½in) lengths of turquoise wire, and a single lime coloured one. Tape them together at one side. Pass a rocaille through the three wires. String a large glass bead onto the first piece, the second, a medium-sized one, and the third, a small pearl. Gather together, and add another rocaille.

6 Next, string on a set of three beads in the same way, always adding a rocaille before and after each section. Attach three more. Gather the wires and pass a large spotted design, and another small bead. Thread three gems and a silver foil design. Add a further set, and a large spotted gem. String on three beads, then pass seven rocailles onto all three wires.

7 Insert the lime coloured wire from the back through the shell flower. String on a large blue green glass bead and a rocaille; and insert back through the glass gem and the motif. Carefully pull taut, and slide into the heart of the embellishment. Finish the other half of the necklace in the same way.

8 Take 75cm (29½in) of turquoise wire, and insert through all fourteen rocailles on the reverse of the flower. Pull both ends even, and finish one half of the necklace as follows: thread on a rocaille and a shell, and insert the wire back through the small bead. Add three more shells, and finish the other side the same way.

9 Remove the tape from the flower motif necklace and string rocailles onto each side, until the desired length is achieved. Repeat this for the shorter design. String a crimp bead onto the ends of each wire. Insert into a jump ring, then pull through the next four or five gems. To secure, flatten the crimps and attach to a fastener.

YOU WILL NEED:
• Special Adult Designer Necklace Kit, includes: wire, beads, shells, findings

Tools:
• Wire cutters
• Pliers, flat-nose

This necklace has a real wow factor, yet it's easier to make than it looks!

Top tip

To strengthen the flower motif, thread wire through all beads twice.

Fashion Statement

Add the perfect finishing touch to your outfit with this gorgeous purse and earring set. Small handbags are very popular at the moment, especially embroidered and beaded examples. Stitch this lovely little purse from shimmering lilac dupion and decorate with co-ordinating gems, which you can also use to make a pair of delightful earrings. You may be inspired to create another set for someone else, in which case we also have a matching card to round off those lovely gifts.

YOU WILL NEED:

Purse:
- Handle, bag, with chain
- Silk dupion, two contrasting colours
- Beads, assorted: rocaille seed; drops; pearl, two shades
- Headpins
- Needle, beading
- Thread, matching

Earrings:
- Chain, silver
- Beads, assorted, as before
- Headpins
- Jump rings
- Earring hooks

Card:
- Card blank, cream
- Silk dupion
- Needle
- Thread
- 3-D foam pads
- Wording
- Adhesive, spray
- Headpin
- Beads

Tools:
- Pliers, three-in-one
- Ruler
- Pencil
- Sewing machine
- Scissors
- Craft knife

Designer
Amanda Walker

Purse

1 From the silk dupion, cut two squares double the width of the bag handle; e.g. if it is 7cm (2¾in) cut two 14cm (5½in) squares. Trace around the inner edge of the handle onto paper then add 5mm (⅛in) to the outer edge. From the centre, measure down 14cm (5½in), and from this point, draw a line that extends 7cm (2¾in) either side, parallel to the top. To complete the pattern, join the two ends of the base to the two ends of the traced outer line. Use this template as a guide and cut two pieces from the remaining contrasting silk to form the purse lining.

2 Lay the two silk squares on top of each other then position the handle onto one corner. Make a pencil mark on the edge of the fabric to indicate where the hinged end comes, and transfer this to the opposite side of the square. Machine stitch from this point to the other, around the base of the fabric, with a 5mm (⅛in) seam allowance. Turn the squares right side out and press the seams flat. Stitch the lining pieces together in the same manner, but leave the bag un-turned.

3 The handle has a row of tiny holes pierced into the metal around the inner edge for attaching the bag. Find the centre top of one side of the purse, thread the needle and stitch this point through the middle hole to the inside of the opened handle. Continue sewing, gathering the silk as you move across the handle. When you turn the corner, the fabric should be attached flat. Stitch as far as the hinged end of the handle and knot the thread securely. The hinge should be just above the end of the machine sewing. Carry on attaching the rest of the silk in the same manner.

4 Place the un-turned lining inside the silk bag. Hand stitch to the handle, again through the tiny holes. As you sew, fold in the raw edges of the fabrics to neaten the inside of the purse. Stitch a tiny rocaille bead to each of the holes on the outside of the handle. To make the droplet on the centre front of the bag, thread a headpin with a seed bead, a drop, another seed, a pale pink pearl, a third seed, a smaller lilac bead and then a final seed. Using the cutter part of the pliers, trim the tip of the pin to leave 1cm protruding from the threaded beads, then bend the top over to form a ring with the tips. Stitch the droplet to the centre hole of the handle.

Top tip

Work in good light on a flat, clear surface to make this project easy on your hands and eyes!

110

Earrings

Cut six lengths of chain: two 3cm (1⅛in); two 2.5cm (1in); and two 2cm (¾in) long. Make up a headpin with beads as in step four for the purse. Trim the top, then thread the end through the chain. Repeat with the five remaining pieces of chain. Open out a jump ring and thread on three sections of chain, one of each length. Thread on an earring hook. Repeat with the remaining components to complete the pair.

Card

1 Trim two squares from silk dupion, one slightly smaller than the other, and fray the edges. Cut another square from paper, slightly smaller than the little silk shape. Using spray adhesive, stick the paper to the back of the fabric, then adhere the larger square to the front of the blank.

2 Make up a beaded headpin as before, and stitch to the centre of the paper-backed silk. Add four foam pads, then fix to the middle of the larger square on the front of the card. Finally, cut your chosen wording from a sheet, or print from a computer, and attach with foam pads below the fabric.

Be catwalk smart with this pretty beaded purse and matching earrings and card

Top tip

These items would make a fab gift set for a special person. Co-ordinate with matching gift-tag and paper.

Simply Elegant

Make sure your jewels stand out in the crowd with this eye-catching necklace. This design features clusters of beads which shimmer and glisten in the light. The faceted and glass pearl beads give an elegant feel, while the strands of gold wire add a delicate touch. Try using different colours to complement whatever you wear!

Top tip

This necklace would look fabulous in a matching gift box.

Designer
Amanda Walker

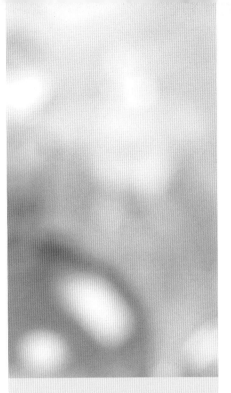

YOU WILL NEED:
- Craft wire, green, 0.5mm (25swg), 0.20mm (36swg)
- Faceted glass beads, 6mm (¼in), 4mm (27swg)
- Glass pearl beads, 12mm (½in)
- Threading jewel, large, round
- Crimp beads, silver
- Calottes, large, silver
- Silver jump rings
- Extender chain with crab claw fastening

Tools:
- Wire cutters
- Flat-nose pliers
- Crimp bead pliers

Try using silver wire with blue crystals for a contrasting look

1 Using the wire cutters cut four 30cm (12in) lengths from the thicker wire. Thread a glass pearl onto the centre of one of these and then a large and a small glass faceted bead and a crimp bead to either side. Squeeze the crimp beads with the crimping pliers to hold them in place.

2 Take another length of wire and repeat the process, this time making two clusters of beads, 4cm (1½in) either side of the centre point.

3 Take the next piece of wire and this time make smaller clusters of one large 6mm (¼in) faceted glass bead and two smaller 4mm (³⁄₁₆in) beads held in place, again with two crimp beads. Position these two clusters 8cm (3in) either side of the centre point.

4 With the final piece of wire make two smaller clusters, but place these 4cm (1½in) either side of the centre point of the wire.

5 Place the beaded wires on top of each other on a flat surface, levelling the ends of the wires. Now arrange the wires, making the wire with the single cluster sit on the outer edge and then place the remaining three one above the other. The ends of the wires will be different lengths now. Pinch the wires together, trim them to the same length, and then thread on a crimp bead. Squeeze the bead around the wires and then, with the flat-nose pliers, bend the ends of the wire over onto themselves. Repeat this process to the other end of the wires.

6 Next, from the finer 0.20mm (36swg) wire, cut six 30cm (12in) lengths. Thread three of these through the top holes of the threading jewel and the remaining three through the base holes, placing the jewel in the centre of the wires.

7 Place the threading jewel in amongst the other prepared wires above the centre cluster. Gather the ends of the wires together and, as before, trim them to the same lengths as the thicker wires, thread on a crimp bead, squeeze, and then bend the ends of the wires over.

8 Place the ends into the two calottes and then squeeze them closed with the flat-nose pliers. Finally open two jump rings and thread one onto each calotte. Before you close the jump rings, thread the crab claw fastening onto one and the extender chain onto the other.

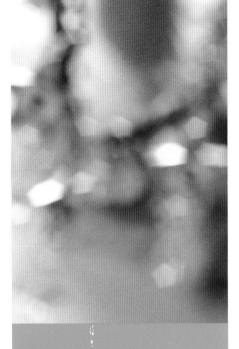

Star Turn

Glam up your evening wear with this stunning set of handmade jewellery When it comes to a range of beads and findings to turn into exciting new projects, silver with blue, pink and mother of pearl is an eye-catching combination. The stylish designs used to make up this gorgeous collection are all co-ordinated so that the pieces can be mixed and matched to suit your mood or outfit. Each component is chosen for ease of use and no special skills are required – just a few basic tools and nimble fingers – making this a great idea for novices to try. With finished results as pretty as these items, what are you waiting for?

YOU WILL NEED:
- Pliers: flat-nose; pointed
- Wire cutters
- Scissors
- Cord, leather, square, blue
- End cap
- Jump rings, 1mm (1⁄16) x 4mm (3⁄16in)
- Beads, glass, pyramid
- Headpin, silver 30mm (1⅕in)
- Ear wires, rings, silver
- Glue, Bison Power
- Chain, round link, 6mm (1⁄4in)
- Clasp, ring and bar, large
- Strass stones, pale amethyst, 2.7mm (1⁄10in)
- Inlaid star, silver

Pearl Bracelet
- Chain, fine link, silver
- Jump rings
- 1mm (1⁄16in) x 4mm (3⁄16in)
- Pyramid glass beads
- Headpin, 30mm (1⅕in), silver
- Ear wires, rings, silver
- Eyepin, 30mm (1⅕in), silver
- Beads, metal
- Shapes, mother-of-pearl, flat

Designer
Amanda Walker

Pearl Bracelet

1 To make the bracelet, first cut a length of silver chain to fit your wrist. Attach a jump ring to each end of the chain, then a hook fastener to one of the rings. Then thread five pyramid glass beads onto the end pins.

2 Cut off the tip of the pin, leaving enough to bend into a ring. Open a jump ring and thread on a glass bead. Then attach the rings to five mother-of-pearl shapes.

3 Now, thread six headpins with a pyramid bead, then a metal one, finishing up with another pyramid. Using a pair of pliers, carefully bend the end of the pin over to form a ring. Next, open out and attach a jump ring to each of the prepared mother-of-pearl shapes and the metal bead pins, then space out and attach evenly around the chain.

Earrings

1 To make the earrings, thread two end pins with pyramid beads, then cut off the ends. Pass the end pins through the ring of two eyepins. Bend the ends over to secure. Carefully thread a pyramid bead onto the eyepin followed by a metal bead. Finish with another pyramid gem. Then bend the top over to form a ring.

2 Repeat with the remaining eyepin, then open two jump rings, and before closing, thread on a mother-of-pearl shape and the beaded eyepins. To complete the pearl earrings attach two earring hooks to the top of each of the shapes using jump rings, as shown.

Be the envy of all your friends with these stylish accessories, perfect for any outfit or occasion

Top tip

Invest in a good pair of pliers and wire cutters – they help with accuracy and dexterity when making jewellery.

116

Blue Stars Necklace

1 Using the wire cutters, trim the chain and leather cord to fit your nexk comfortably. Fix an end cap to the tips of the cord.

2 Open a jump ring and thread it to the ring of the end cap, and then to the last link of the chain. Before closing the jump ring, attach the bar of the clasp. Repeat this process to the ends of the cord and chain, except this time, attach the ring of the clasp.

3 Make up 17 end pins using blue pyramid beads. Cut off the tip of each pin, leaving enough to bend into a ring (1cm (½in)). Open the jump ring and thread on the glass bead. Hook the jump ring to the end cap, then pinch closed. Open another jump ring and push on three glass beads. Fix to the base of the star. Arrange on the centre link of the chain and around the length of cord.

4 Make up four more clusters of three beads and attach two on either side of the centre star. Add a single gem to two stars and fix either side of the clusters. Finish by attaching the remaining two clusters in place. Add an amethyst stone to the centre of each star.

Earrings

1 Make up two clusters of pyramid beads, then fix to the base of two stars with jump rings.

2 Attach these to the top of each star and add earring hooks. Finally, stick an amethyst stone to the centre of each star. Your dazzling earrings will now be ready to wear!

Top tip

When applying end clasps, pinch one side of the fastener at a time with your fingers.

Patterns and diagrams

Iced Gems (page 42)

Making a headpin

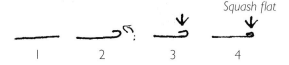

Squash flat

1	2	3	4

Making a link

1   2

Making tassels

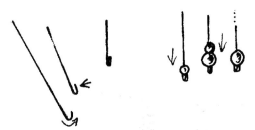

Making up

Making a loop in the bauble

Squeeze crimp

More Gems (page 54)

W — — X

Z — — Y

Diagram 1
(note, four beads either side are not shown)

A   B

Diagram 2
Flat surface of beading

Simply Charming (page 90)

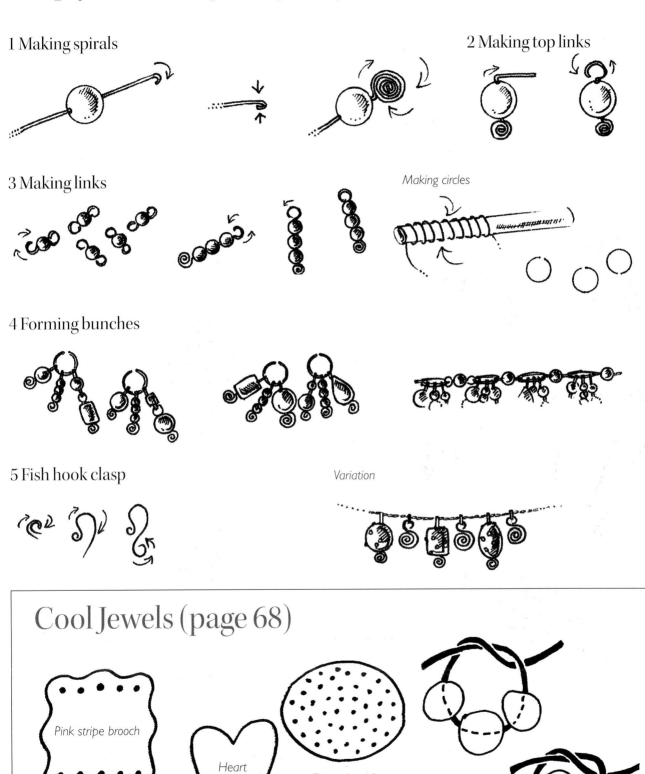

1 Making spirals

2 Making top links

3 Making links

Making circles

4 Forming bunches

5 Fish hook clasp

Variation

Cool Jewels (page 68)

Pink stripe brooch

Heart brooch

Flower brooch

Where to buy

Sparkle and Shine, Gillian Slone, page 30
- Bead Addict, 0161 973 1945,
  www.beadaddict.com
- Grove Beads, www.grovebeads.co.uk
For beads and accessories

Heart's Desire, Jema Hewitt, page 34
- Bead Shop, 21a Tower St, London, WC2H 9NS, 020 7240 0931,
  www.beadworks.co.uk,
- Mail order, The Bead shop, 0115 9588899,
  www.mailorder-beads.co.uk
For all items used in this project

Perfect Timing, Atelier Rayher, page 38
- Clark Craft Products, 08000 371420, www.clarkcraft.co.uk
- Embsay Crafts, 0113 2624091, www.embsaycrafts.co.uk
- Rayher, www.rayher-hobby.de
For all materials used in this project

Mint Finish, EFCO Hobbies, page 40
- Sinotex Ltd, 01737 245450, www.sinotex.co.uk
For EFCO Hobby silver-plated bracelet blank, heart pendant blank, Swarovski crystals, and silver-lined Indian beads

Iced Gems, Linda Jones, page 42
- Beads, Creative Bead Craft, 01494 778818,
  www.creativebeadcraft.co.uk

Bead Dazzle, Amanda Walker, page 46
- Kars stockists (including Craftability), 01525 875798, www.kars.biz
For all components used to make these items

Crown Jewels, Jema Hewitt, page 50
- The Bead Shop, 104-106 Upper Parliament St,
  Nottingham, NG1 6LF, 01159 588899, www.mailorderbeads.co.uk
For tiara bands, beads and wire
- The Bead Shop, 21a Tower St, London, WC2H 9NS,
  www.beadworks.co.uk

More Gems, Gillian Slone, page 54
- Gillian Slone, 01723 516107, www.beadography.co.uk
For kits containing everything you need for these projects

Razzle Dazzle, Lucinda Ganderton, page 58
- Gütermann stockists, 0208 589 1653
For rectangular blue, faceted amber and turquoise matte beads
- The Bead Shop, 020 7240 0931
For clear bead elastic and iridescent green beads

Bead Sparkling, Corinne Bradd, page 60
- Createa Crafts Limited, 01782 210651, www.creata-crafts.co.uk

Oriental Charm, Jema Hewitt, page 64
- The Bead Shop, 104–106 Upper Parliament St, Nottingham,
  NG1 6LF, 01159 588899, www.mailorderbeads.co.uk
- The Bead Shop, 21a Tower St, London, WC2H 9NS,
  www.beadworks.co.uk
- Hobbycraft stores nationwide, 0800 027 2387,
  www.hobbycraft.co.uk
For stamps and sculpey

Cool Jewels, Glennis Gilruth, page 68
- Creative Films Ltd, 0845 4534 831
For Holographic plastic sheets
- Hobbycraft, stores nationwide, 0800 027 2387,
  www.hobbycraft.co.uk
For plastic beads, clear monofilament by Impex, and Beadalon Elasticity clear bead cord

Busy Beads, Dorothy Wood, page 76
- Gütermann suppliers., 0208 589 1600
For beads, jewellery findings, tools and wire,
- John Lewis, 08456 049049
For a selection of beads
- HobbyCraft stores nationwide, 0800 027 2387,
  www.hobbycraft.co.uk
For a selection of beads

Charm School, Alison Galpin, page 84
- EP Beads, 01246 556988, www.epbeads.co.uk
For all components used to make these items

Good Times, Corinne Bradd, page 88
- Craftability, 01525 875798, www.craft-ability.com
For Kars beads and jewellery making items

Simply Charming, Linda Jones, page 90
- Jillybeads, 01524 412728, www.jillybeads.co.uk
For 'Bobbly' beads
- Beadcraft, 01494 778818, www.creativebeadcraft.co.uk
For creative wire
- Empirical Praxis, 01246 556988, www.epbeads.co.uk
For creative wire

Pearly Queen, Dorothy Wood, page 98
- Rayher, www.rayher-hobby.de, email info@rayher-hobby.de
For all beads and findings

Flower Power, Margo Van Engelen, page 106
- Email info@avec.nl
For a Special Adult Designer Necklace Kit

Fashion Statement, Amanda Walker, page 108
- Kars - visit www.kars.biz for stockist details
For bag handle, beads and jewellery findings
- MacCulloch and Wallis Ltd, 020 7629 0311,
  www.macculloch-wallis.co.uk
For silk dupion

Star Turn, Amanda Walker, page 114
- Kars - visit www.kars.biz for stockist details
For all materials used in this project

Index